The Great

And Not So Great

Love Stories

of the Bible

King Duncan

ISBN: 0-936497-64-5
Seven Worlds Publishing
1004 Reunion Drive
Chattanooga, TN 37421

Unless otherwise noted, all scriptures are from the New International Version (NIV) Copyright (c) 1973, 1978, 1984 by International Bible Society.

Other books by
King Duncan
From Seven Worlds
The One-Minute Motivator
Amusing Grace
Help! I've Fallen Down Laughing and I Can't Get Up

Also
By
King Duncan
The Amazing Law of Influence:
How You Can Change Your World
(Pelican Press)

Contents

**For other books and resources by
King Duncan**
please go to
www.sevenworldspub.com

SEVEN WORLDS
PUBLISHING

To Selina—
The love of my life

Special thanks to Angela Akers
for her invaluable assistance
in making these stories come alive

INTRODUCTION

I love a good story. Charles Dickens once said that a good story should make you laugh, make you cry, and make you worry.

The Bible is an amazing collection of stories. Some of these stories will make you laugh. Others will make you cry. Some will not only make you worry, they will outright shock you, even if you think you already know them well. The Bible describes real life, as it was lived 2,000 to 3,500 years ago. Out of the stories of real people, God will speak to you.

Sometime back, I read a hilarious story on the Internet. It was about a missionary to Haiti. He had served there many years ago and was telling about his experience. He said the worst part of being a missionary is learning the language. He remarked that it's miserable when you're unable to communicate the most basic aspects of life, from "where's the bathroom?" to "how much do you want for that mango?" In no time at all, you feel like the stupidest person on the face of the earth.

One time, he said, he told the yard boy, "Remember, I am garbage" instead of "Remember to take out my garbage."

It was even worse when he would try to share his faith with someone. The first conversation he had along those lines went like this: "If you accept Jesus Christ, he will take away your dogs."

"My dogs?" the person asked, "I don't have any dogs."

"Everyone has dogs, ma'am," he said, continuing his

presentation without a clue that he was using the word for "dogs" rather than the word for "sins."

"But when Jesus forgives them," he said with finality, "it's as though you never had a dog your entire life."

He tells about Bill Smith, an Assemblies of God missionary in Haiti, who once instructed a church congregation that if anyone wanted to become followers of Christ, they should signify it by raising their legs into the air and coming forward on their hands.

"There were lots of puzzled looks," he says, "but very little response to the altar call."

One of the funniest stories he tells is about Dale Preiser, another Assemblies of God missionary. The word Dale had wanted to use on this occasion was "mambo," which means a voodoo priestess. Instead he said "mamba," which is the word for peanut butter. He gave several impassioned sermons about the dangers of Christians consulting with peanut butter in times of need. He reports that sales of peanut butter did fall in the area for a while. [1]

It's not easy to communicate with someone who speaks a different language. I have an Austrian son-in-law. Fortunately, he speaks impeccable English. My wife and I speak no German, which is the official language of Austria. When we visit with his parents, who speak no English, it makes for an awkward situation. Making signals with your hands will only take you so far. It makes me feel like Zechariah after he came out of the temple where he was struck speechless while people were waiting for him to address them in behalf of the Lord. We'll deal with his dilemma later in the book.

Communication is a difficult process. It is difficult to communicate with another person. Now, imagine trying to communicate with another species. Tell the mosquito, as it flies around your arm, that your spouse is much tastier than you are. Good luck with that.

Here's where I am leading: imagine the Creator of the universe trying to communicate with you and me. It's like you and me trying to communicate with a mosquito.

God is beyond space and time. With our little brains, we can't even imagine a world without space and time. We say God is Spirit. What does that mean, really? Beats me. *The only thing we know about God is what God chooses to reveal.* That is what the Bible is all about.

The Bible is not a book of theology. Theology is, of course, the study of God. How absurd. We have the capacity to study mosquitoes. Imagine mosquitoes coming together to study us. They might come together to bite us, but to understand us? That's absurd. It is about as absurd as saying that we can capture the nature of God in our little box of a brain.

The Bible is not a book of theology but of revelation. God wanted to communicate with human creatures. How does God do that considering our pathetic ability to understand? Through story–through picture–through the life experiences of human beings–and when God couldn't do it any other way, God *became* story in Jesus Christ. "Tell me the stories of Jesus . . ."

God became a human being who walked among us and revealed Himself to us. And, in the person of Jesus Christ, God taught. And how did he teach? Through stories.

Jesus could have given us a lecture on salvation, instead he told us about a father who had two sons, and the younger of them said "Give me my share of the inheritance . . ."—the parable of the prodigal son. (Luke 15:11-31)

He could have written us a treatise on social responsibility. Instead, he told a story about a man who was going down from Jerusalem to Jericho, when he fell into the hands of robbers. They stripped him of his clothes, beat him and went away, leaving him half dead—the story of the Good Samaritan (Luke 10: 25-37).

The Bible is God's attempt to reach out to us. God does that through story. The Bible is primarily a story book. It also contains laws and precepts, of course. But rarely do these connect with us in quite the way that the stories do. If you want to know what God expects out of God's highest creation, which is humanity, read the stories of the Bible.

We call this little book, *The Great and Not So Great Love Stories of the Bible*. Of course there is only one truly *great* love story in the Bible. It begins like this: "God so loved the world . . ." That's the only truly great love story. All the other biblical love stories are imperfect—for several good reasons.

For one thing, Bible people are imperfect, just as you and I are imperfect. The Bible is starkly candid about the imperfection of human nature. These imperfections grow out of what the Bible calls sin. This sinfulness is on display in most of the relationships we will encounter. Imperfect people simply are not capable of perfect relationships.

Of course, the status of women in biblical times also made authentic relationships quite difficult. Some of the patriarchs had multiple marriages. This was a time when arranged marriages were the norm. Romantic love is a fairly recent development in human history. In these more primitive times, life was hard as well as short. Marriages were often a matter of convenience.

For example, there was a tradition that if a man died, his brother was to marry the man's wife. In doing this he both continued the family line and the widow was provided for. If you are a woman, imagine being forced into a marriage with your brother-in-law, without regard to what your sister-in-law might think of the arrangement. Things could get a little messy.

So, the great love stories contained in the pages of the Bible might not match up to contemporary expectations. And some of the stories are actually quite shocking, as we have already noted—but none are boring. And yet out of these stories God still speaks in a marvelous way to our limited and sinful brains.

So let's get started. But where shall we begin? At the beginning, of course, with the first woman and the first man.

ADAM AND EVE
Genesis 1:26-5:5

Someone once asked the internationally known preacher and theologian, Dr. Carlyle Marney, where the Garden of Eden was.

He replied, "215 East Elm Street, Knoxville, Tennessee."

"What?" gasped the questioner. "I thought it was in Mesopotamia."

"Well," Dr. Marney drawled, "you couldn't prove it by me. It was there on Elm Street, when I was a boy, that I stole a quarter out of Mama's purse and ran to the store and bought a bag of peanut clusters and ate it as fast as I could. Afterward, I was so ashamed that I came back home to 215 Elm Street and hid in the closet. Mama found me and asked, 'Why are you hiding? What have you done?'"

That amazed me when I read that the Garden of Eden was at 215 East Elm Street, Knoxville, Tennessee, because I had always believed that it was at Rt. 14, Badgett Road, also in Knoxville. I was five or six years old and I had just hit my cousin John in the head with a rock. I hid in the attic of our house and listened to my aunt tell my mother what a monster I was.

The story of Adam and Eve is *our* story. It is not simply the story of one woman and one man; it is the story of us all; your story, as well as mine.

God lovingly creates a garden world with every good thing to eat. And God places us in it. God gives us everything we need to thrive in this world, including other people to live with and to love. And what do we do? We foul it up. Invariably, we foul it up.

Why do we do the things we do? We'll deal with that a little later. But it's in our DNA. My wife is continually asking me, "why did you do that?" or, "why did you say that?"

I shrug my shoulders. Sometimes I don't even know why I do some of the things I do. And some of the things I've done make me cringe when I think of them. That's why we need to take a fresh look at this old, old story of the first man and the first woman. It's our story.

The story begins with Adam. It's interesting. The Scriptures tell us that originally God spoke everything into existence: "God said, 'Let there be light,' and there was light . . . And God said, 'Let there be a vault between the waters to separate water from water' . . . Then God said, 'Let the land produce vegetation . . .' And God said, 'Let there be lights in the vault of the sky to separate the day from the night . . .'" (Genesis 1). God spoke everything into existence—except human beings. God fashioned us with His own hands.

Think about that for a moment. The first few chapters of the Bible tell a story of wondrous intimacy—between God and human beings, between the first man and the first woman, and even between humanity and the environment. At least, that was God's intent.

Adam has a partner. Her name is Eve. The Scriptures say they were created in God's own image. Adam and Eve live in a beautiful garden. They live in perfect partnership. Eve was taken from Adam's side and at his side is her rightful place. The subjugation of woman comes *after* their expulsion from the Garden of Eden.

Adam's response, when he first beholds Eve is one of utter surprise and joy. We're told that the English translation cannot adequately express the full measure of Adam's delight as he gazes upon this lovely creature that God has provided to him to be his soul mate, but it's something like, "Wow!"

Adam pronounces his name and hers, *Ish* and *Isshah*. The author of Genesis goes on to write, "for this reason, a man will leave his father and mother and be united to his wife, and they will become one flesh" (Gen 2:24).

One flesh. Equal in every way. Different, but equal. Vive la différence!

Someone has noted that, "ninety percent of the people in jail are men, while ninety percent of the people in counseling are women."

Yes, we are different.

Actress Katharine Hepburn once commented, "Sometimes, I wonder if men and women really suit each other. Perhaps they should live next door and just visit now and then."

Different, but equal. In Genesis 2:20 Eve is referred to as a "suitable helper" for Adam (NIV). The Hebrew word used for "suitable helper" is *ezer*. One scholar has noted that this same word, *ezer*, is used to identify God as man's helper in Psalm 33:20 and other passages in the Bible. So Eve's stature with regard to Adam is clearly not intended to be inferior if God can also be man's helper.

And they were naked. They had no problem with self-acceptance. They had nothing to hide. Imagine relationships without emotional baggage from the past. Imagine sex without shame or fear.

God created Adam and Eve to "be fruitful and multiply." Someone has said that this is the only command that humanity has obeyed.

David A. Macleod wrote in *Reader's Digest* about his son's wedding to a lovely Russian woman. At the reception, guests toasted the couple with a number of traditional American and Russian toasts. One American woman offered this warm wish: "Good health, good fortune. Go and multiply."

When this toast was translated, it met with puzzled looks from many of the Russian guests. The translator had re-worded the toast to say, "Good health, and good fortune. Go and do math." [2]

God created sex to be joyful, natural, and intimate. Need I say that sex is just one more thing of which humanity has made a mess.

Adam and Eve were forbidden from only one thing—the fruit from a tree in the center of the garden—the Tree of the Knowledge of Good and Evil. The Scriptures do not say it was an apple tree, but it doesn't hurt to visualize the forbidden fruit as a big, juicy Golden Delicious. God told Adam and Eve that they could eat the fruit of any tree in the garden except that one.

Some cynic has said that it wasn't the apple on the tree but the pair on the ground that started all our troubles.

Mark Twain once said that God's mistake was not making the snake forbidden—for then Adam would have eaten it.

But one day Eve is walking in the garden. And she sees the

forbidden fruit and, at the urging of the serpent, she takes one little bite.

Isn't that how it so often begins? One small violation of our values. Sometimes it's as insignificant as a phone call. Or one small discrepancy on an expense voucher. Or one small puff of an illegal substance. Someone has put it this way:

> *"Who's there?" I cried.*
> *"A little lonely sin."*
> *"Enter," I said.*
> *And all hell was in.*

Eve took a bite from the forbidden fruit. And then, to compound her error, she gave a bite to Adam. And so Eve has been blamed since time immemorial for leading Adam into sin.

But note how the story actually reads, "when the woman saw that the fruit of the tree was good for food and pleasing to the eye, and also desirable for gaining wisdom, she took some and ate it. She also gave some to her husband, **who was with her**, and he ate it." (Gen. 3:6, emphasis added).

Adam was with Eve when she ate the forbidden fruit, yet Adam does nothing to intervene. He watches Eve take and eat the forbidden fruit even though God has told him that if they eat of the fruit they shall surely die. Only after he sees that Eve has eaten of the fruit and is still alive does he take the fruit from her and munches on the apple himself. Adam was at least an accessory to Eve's crime.

When God confronts Adam about his misdeed, he, being a typical husband, tries to put the blame on Eve. But God knows better. Adam had been there when Eve ate the fruit. He could have stopped her if he had chosen. Still, they both violated God's command, and now they both must pay.

As the great missionary E. Stanley Jones used to say, "We don't break God's laws; we break ourselves on those laws."

The first casualty of their misdoing was loss of innocence. The Bible tells us the eyes of both of them were opened, and they knew that they were naked, and they sewed fig leaves together and made themselves loincloths. From this time forward, comedian Joey Adams once quipped, "They argued over who would wear the plants in the family."

The innocent Adam and Eve discover what it means to be

naked. Exposed. Ashamed.

The story is told about one of the early pioneer missionaries who were sent to the Aymara people in Bolivia. By our standards, the Aymara walk around quite naked. The men wear only a thin fiber string around their waist. It really doesn't cover anything of importance, but this string is very important to them.

This missionary, a woman, tells of visiting a sick man in his hut to bring him medication. "As she entered his home, he made signs of extreme embarrassment. He fidgeted nervously, moving about the shelter and calling for assistance from his wife. She ran in, bringing his string, and tied it around his waist. As soon as the string was in place, the man relaxed. After that, he was able to speak with ease and confidence with this Western woman—even though to her he was not really covered up at all. From his perspective, however, he was no longer naked." [3]

Adam and Eve suddenly discover they are naked. And with the loss of innocence comes a loss of intimacy. Nothing will ever again be the same for this couple, and subsequently for all people. We simply cannot overemphasize the brokenness that comes into human relations from this day forward.

We particularly see this brokenness when Adam and Eve begin having children. As the old joke says, what was the first thing that Adam and Eve did after God expelled them from the Garden of Eden? They raised Cain!

They named their first two sons, Cain and Abel. And all hell breaks loose. Life east of Eden is no longer a picture of intimacy and love. In Genesis 4, we read of history's first homicide. In a fit of jealousy, Cain attacks his brother Abel and kills him.

Tragically, this conflict establishes a pattern for subsequent relationships between siblings in Genesis: Isaac versus Ishmael, Esau versus Jacob, and Joseph versus his brothers—every one of these relationships is a disaster! But we're getting ahead of the story.

Ignoring God's command changes everything in Adam and Eve's life. Even the serpent is caught up in the aftermath of their misdeed. God decrees that it crawl on its belly, and eat dust all the days of its life. This punishment is affirmed in the messianic prophecy in Isaiah 65:25, "the wolf and the lamb will feed together and the lion will eat straw like the ox. But dust will be the serpent's food."

To Eve, God says, "I will greatly increase your pains in childbearing; with pain you will give birth to children. Your desire will be for your husband, and he will rule over you."

Here's an interesting question for you to ponder: are these truly curses which God placed upon the woman or are these merely a *description* of how life will be in a fallen world? For example, suppose modern science were to eliminate all pain in childbirth? Would that mean that we have eliminated God's curse?

And how about woman's subjection to man? Is that a curse or is it simply a description of the way things are in a fallen world?

Actually, this question is academic, because Christ has removed the curse from Eve, as well as from all womanhood. St. Paul, not exactly regarded as a feminist, writes in Galatians 3:28, "there is neither Jew nor Greek, slave nor free, **male nor female**, for you are all one in Christ Jesus."

To Adam, God says, "Cursed is the ground because of you; through painful toil you will eat of it all the days of your life. It will produce thorns and thistles for you, and you will eat the plants of the field. By the sweat of your brow you will eat your food until you return to the ground, since from it you were taken; for dust you are and to dust you will return."

Notice that it is not the man who is cursed, but the ground. Man already had been given dominion over the garden. He was already responsible for its upkeep. But now it will no longer be a joy to maintain. The loss of intimacy not only extended to Eve, but even to the earth from which Adam had come. Now life would be "toil." The Hebrew word for *toil* is the same word that is used for the pain that the woman will experience in childbearing.

Here again, is this a curse or a description? Many men love their work, as do many women. Other things are actually much more like the pain of childbirth than going to the office each day. (Then again—I don't know your boss.) Of course, if you are a woman, you are probably gritting your teeth and mumbling, "he doesn't know. No pain can be compared to childbirth." And I don't know. But still, I have difficulty believing that the idea of a curse being visited on all women because of Eve's sin is to be taken literally.

There is a fourth punishment, the most deadly of them all, which is visited on both Adam and Eve. They are banished from the

Garden of Eden, "so the Lord God banished him from the Garden of Eden to work the ground from which he had been taken. After he drove the man out, he placed on the east side of the Garden of Eden cherubim and a flaming sword flashing back and forth to guard the way to the tree of life." (Gen. 3:24)

And that's where many people live today—East of Eden, in a state of brokenness, estrangement and shame. Why did the first man and woman sin? Why do you and I sin?

Well, somebody says, "the devil made me do it."

Wrong answer, unless you are Flip Wilson's Geraldine.

"Why did you buy the new dress?"

"Well, honey, the devil made me does it."

"Didn't you say, 'Get thee behind me Satan?'"

"Yeah, but he said it looked good in back, too."

Bad theology. The devil can't make you do anything. As pastor Chuck Smoot notes, "All throughout Scripture we see that the devil does one thing. He tempts. He tricks. He cajoles. He makes applications. But we see, that in every case, the devil offers, for lack of a better word, an opportunity, and it is up to us to accept or reject it.

"And even if we look at his actions in the book of Job, we notice something very interesting. The devil actually didn't do anything. All the devil did was talk to and challenge God. God did all of the things that happened to Job, both physically and with his possessions. When the devil tempted Jesus, that was all he did, which is why we call it 'the temptation of Christ.'" [4]

So, don't blame the devil. You and I are responsible for our own actions.

It's like a story that Anthony Evans tells about an old forester named Sam. As Old Sam was out chopping down trees, he would moan: "Oh, Adam. Oh, Adam." Every time he hit that tree, he'd say, "Oh, Adam."

One day the foreman came by and asked him, "How come every time you hit the tree, you say, 'Oh, Adam'?"

Sam said, "Because Adam, my forefather, sinned against God. God cursed him and said that he would have to work from that time on. So every time I hit this ax against the tree, it reminds me that if Adam hadn't sinned, I wouldn't have to work."

One day, Sam's supervisor took him to his big, plush, palatial ten-thousand-square-foot mansion.

He said, "It's all yours. You can live in it; you can do whatever you want. You've got a swimming pool, a tennis court, servants—everything. Everything in this house is yours. I'm giving it to you because I don't want you to struggle with that Adam mentality. I ask only one thing: Don't lift up the box on the dining room table. Enjoy everything else in the house. Be what you want to be, do your own thing, but that box on the dining room table, do not touch."

Sam said, "No problem. I can handle it."

So Sam played tennis every day, went swimming, ate three meals a day. But after a few months, he saw that box. It bothered him. He wanted to know why, if he can have everything else, that box was off-limits. He said, "No, I'm not going to touch it; I'm not going to jeopardize my time here."

After a year he had tried everything in the house. There was nothing new anymore. There was only one thing new in that house, and that was that box. And so one day, when nobody was looking, he lifted up the box just a little bit. Out of that box ran a little, teeny mouse that hid, and Sam couldn't catch it and couldn't find it.

The supervisor came and noted that the box had been lifted. He went to Sam and said, "Now Sam, I warned you. Go back out into the forest and pick up your ax and chop again."

The next time the supervisor came by he heard Sam saying, "Oh, Sam. Oh, Sam." [5]

Don't blame the serpent. The fault, dear Brutus, lies within us.

A better question is, did God know that Adam and Eve would sin? And the answer would have to be yes, God knew. God gives us freedom, but God knows our hearts. If God did not give us freedom and allow us to experience the consequences of that freedom, we would remain forever infantile. Freedom and failure seem to be essential to emotional and spiritual growth.

The Apostle Paul in Romans 5 gives us the best explanation for why God created a world in which the possibility of sin exists: "Suffering produces endurance, and endurance produces character, and character produces hope, and hope does not disappoint us" (3-4).

So, ever since the first man and woman we have lived East of Eden, in a world of brokenness and estrangement. God puts an angel with a flaming sword at the entrance of the Garden of Eden so that

Adam and Eve cannot return.

But it doesn't have to be that way for you and me.

There are three gardens of note in Scripture. One, of course, is Eden, where humanity first cried out, "Not your will, but mine be done."

The second is Gethsemane, where a lonely figure cries out, "Not my will but thine be done." There Jesus hangs on a cross. And like the original Adam, he is naked but not ashamed. He is suffering on our behalf so that the curse of death may be removed.

There is a final garden of importance to us. It is at end of the Bible, in the very last chapter of Revelation: "Then the angel showed me the river of the water of life, as clear as crystal, flowing from the throne of God and of the Lamb down the middle of the great street of the city. On each side of the river stood the tree of life, bearing twelve crops of fruit, yielding its fruit every month. And the leaves of the tree are for the healing of the nations. No longer will there be any curse. The throne of God and of the Lamb will be in the city, and his servants will serve him." (Rev. 22:1-3)

In Christ, the curse of death has been removed. Christ has made it possible for innocence and intimacy to be restored. This is the truly Great Love Story that weaves its way through Scripture: God's love for sinful humanity. But there is much for us to learn about life East of Eden that will help us appreciate what God has done in our behalf. And so we move on to the next great love story of the Bible, Abraham and Sarah.

ABRAHAM AND SARAH

Genesis 11: 26-23: 1

God's plan got off to a happy beginning
But Adam ruined it by sinning!
I hope the whole story
Will end in God's glory,
But right now the wrong side is winning. [6]

Life and love are a little more difficult East of Eden. There is no better example than the story of Abraham and Sarah. We are now 1,700 to 2,000 years before the time of Jesus. God came to a man named Abram and gave him a command and a promise: "Go from your country and your kindred and your father's house to the land that I will show you. I will make of you a great nation, and I will bless you, and make your name great, so that you will be a blessing. I will bless those who bless you, and the one who curses you I will curse; and in you all the families of the earth shall be blessed."

And then we read one of the most important statements in all sacred literature: "So Abram went, as the Lord had told him . . ."

It would be impossible to overstate the significance of this step of faith for the subsequent history of the world. This, by the way, is what faith is. God speaks, we obey. We don't say, "I've got to bury my father." We don't say, "I can't afford it." We don't say, "My friends in Sunday School won't approve." God speaks. We obey. Faith is much,

much more than belief. The Scriptures say that even the demons believe (James 2:19). Faith is action.

There was a saint in the sixth century named, ironically, St. Abraham. He was the antithesis of Abraham, the patriarch of our faith. The night before his wedding day, St. Abraham evidently got cold feet and headed to the desert. (He obviously had some serious issues regarding relationships.) For the next fifty years St. Abraham walled himself up in the cell of a monastery. He gave away all his clothing to the poor except a cloak, a goat skin, a bowl, and a map. His only contact with the rest of humanity was a small opening he left for food.

Finally after fifty years, a Bishop talked St. Abraham into going to preach to a neighboring village. And he was an instant success. But for fifty years he wasted his life walled up in his cell in the monastery. That is not faith.

You may object to my characterizing his life in a monastery as a waste. That's a value judgment, I realize. A life of prayer and meditation cannot be easily dismissed. Still, I believe that Christian living requires balance. It requires both prayer and active participation in the community at large. The biblical patriarch Abraham was a man of both prayer and action.

Abraham—or Abram as he was known when we first encounter him—was a wealthy landowner living in Ur, in Mesopotamia, in the north of what is now Iraq. He had family, friends, an honored place in the community. But when God called, he left all that behind. Even more important for our discussion, he asked his wife Sarah, or Sarai as she was known then, to leave all that behind as well. It is not the first time, nor the last, that someone has asked his or her spouse to accompany them in following a vision.

Sarai's faith in Abram may have been as strong in its own way as Abram's faith in God. She left security, social status, a comfortable lifestyle, as well as her family ties to follow her husband. Surely she had doubts about this adventure. And for many years her doubts were justified.

As soon as Abram and Sarai moved to Canaan, a famine hit. It could not have been easy for them, but they were devoted to one another and to God, and so they survived. God looked after Abram as God had promised. But Abram was still no great shakes as a husband. It is a good thing that his faith was reckoned to him as righteousness, as the New Testament tells us, because his own righteousness sometimes left much to be desired.

It's like something that actress Marlo Thomas once said about her husband, TV host Phil Donahue: "I'm married to the best husband in the world . . . and he's nothing to write home about."

Sarai could echo those heartfelt words. In order to escape the famine in Canaan, Abram and Sarai headed for Egypt. And Abram, this great man of faith, became afraid. Sarai was such a beautiful woman, he was afraid that someone in Egypt would do him harm in order to take Sarai away from him. And so he passed her off as his sister. (Actually scholars tell us she was his half-sister; same father, different mothers. They had different values back then.)

Abram even allowed Sarai to become part of Pharaoh's harem. This great man of faith used his wife Sarai to ensure his own safety. Shame on him! He and Sarai became wealthy from their ploy, but the Egyptian Pharaoh and his household were cursed because of Abram's treachery. Why God punished Pharaoh rather than Abram is a puzzle. Some things in Scripture are beyond our understanding.

Even after Abram and Sarai left Egypt, there were problems. There was constant quarreling between the herdsmen of Lot, Abram's nephew, and the herdsmen of Abram. And then, to top that—since they were in the Middle East—of course, there was constant war.

And yet at each turn of the road, Sarai stayed by Abram's side. One can argue that women like Sarai had no power in their relationship, that she was forced to go along with everything that Abram did. And there is probably some truth to that. But it is also likely that Sarai trusted Abram. She knew him intimately and seemingly loved him deeply in spite of his faults. And because she loved him, she chose to trust him, even when his decisions were hurtful or made no sense. Abram had faith in God. Sarai had faith in Abram.

And they made their marriage work—not because they were perfect people, but because of their faith in God and their love for one another. When two people go through serious adversity trusting God and one another, they often develop a deeper, stronger, more honest love for each other than they might have experienced in an "easier" relationship.

Abram and Sarai developed a special kind of relationship. That is why it hurt Sarai so badly that she could not give Abram a son and heir. Sarai was barren, which was considered a curse and dishonor on the family. Children were regarded as a necessity in those days. Who would help with the daily chores if you had no children? Who would look after you in your less-than-golden years? Women who produced no children were regarded as "less of a woman" in the eyes of others.

Sarai knew that Abram loved her, in spite of her barrenness. He could have left her long ago. This lack of children was a heartbreak they shared together.

Sarai's barrenness, however, presented Abram with a faith problem as well. God had promised to make a great nation of him—and he and Sarai could not even seem to produce one child. Maybe this is what caused them to make a grievous error.

Abram and Sarai are getting up in years. Abram's in his 80s; Sarai's in her 70s—and still barren. Sarai's biological . . . um, sundial . . . stopped ticking long ago. So Abram and Sarai decide to use a surrogate. That's what we would call it nowadays. Except there was no artificial means by which this could be done. They would accomplish it the old-fashioned way. They determine that Abram would have a son by an Egyptian slave woman named Hagar. When they did this, they set the stage for one of the saddest stories in all the Scriptures . . . and maybe all of history.

Let's say a word about Hagar, the slave girl. She is not simply a "nobody." In fact, did you realize that Hagar is the only woman in the Bible to receive a promise from God that she would have descendants (Gen 16:7-14)? And she is also the only person in the Old Testament—male or female—ever to call God by name, "You are El-roi, or God of my vision." [9]

Hagar is a flesh-and-blood human being with dreams and ambitions of her own. One of the lessons of this story is, don't treat people like they are objects. It'll come back to bite you. That's how Abram and Sarai treat Hagar. Like an object. She was a slave. She could hardly refuse their desire to use her womb for their personal aspirations. That is the nature of slavery. Slave women were often abused by their male owners.

So Abram slept with Hagar and she conceived. It should not surprise us that relations between Sarai and Hagar immediately headed south. As soon as Hagar realized she was pregnant, she grew to despise Sarai.

And Sarai grew to despise Hagar in return. Sarai began to mistreat Hagar. Unable to bear Sarai's cruelty any longer, Hagar flees to the desert. The writer of Genesis tells us that the angel of the Lord found Hagar near a spring in the desert. And the angel said, "Hagar, servant of Sarai, where have you come from, and where are you going?"

"I'm running away from my mistress Sarai," she answered. And the angel told Hagar to go back to her mistress. In return, Hagar received the divine promise: "I will so increase your descendants that they will be too numerous to count."

The rest of the promise that the angel made to Hagar may sound like a mixed bag to us. Read it for yourself. It's somewhat amusing.

"You are now with child and you will have a son. You shall name him Ishmael, for the Lord has heard of your misery. He will be a **wild donkey of a man** (emphasis added); his hand will be against everyone and everyone's hand against him, and he will live in hostility toward all his brothers."

Interesting prophecy. More about that later. But Hagar seemed to have been satisfied with God's answer. This is when she calls God by name, El-roi, God of my vision.

And thus a son is born of eighty-six-year old Abram and the much younger slave girl Hagar. And they name him "Ishmael" as the angel instructed. *Ishmael* literally means "God hears." The birth of Ishmael is an important historical event as we shall soon see.

But let's return to Abram and Sarai.

The day came when God changed Abram's name to Abraham and Sarai's name to Sarah. And God made them a promise, that in spite of their advanced years they would have a child. This is quite a remarkable story.

Three men (presumably angels) visit Abraham in the heat of the early afternoon. Hospitality is a cardinal virtue in the Middle East so Abraham bids them to stay, washes their feet, enlists the help of Sarah and the servants in preparing a meal for them. One of the visitors inquires after Sarah and announces that at this time next year, she would bear a son. At this point we read: "Sarah laughed to herself, saying, 'After I have grown old, and my husband is old, shall I have pleasure?'"

"Shall I have pleasure" is a euphemism. It implies sexual pleasure. It's an example of the earthiness of the Old Testament. No wonder Sarah laughs! When the stranger rebukes her for laughing, she is embarrassed, and denies it.

Early Christian theologians were fond of discovering events in the Old Testament that they believed prefigured events in the New Testament. Thus they saw in this encounter of Abraham and the three strangers a visitation not of three angels, but a visitation from God in three persons—Father, Son and Holy Spirit. That may be stretching things a little bit. But theologians are prone to stretch things. It's much easier, however, to accept the men as angels—which means simply, "messengers of God."

So, Abraham and Sarah are left to wait on the birth of their son. Times of waiting can be an opportunity for blessings or a curse. If in our waiting we become bitter or lose our faith, then we will miss a great opportunity to grow in the grace of God.

Author Sue Monk Kidd confesses that she cannot stand to wait. She learned a lesson about the value of waiting on God from a monk who told her: "When you are waiting you are not doing nothing. You're doing something. You're allowing your soul to grow up. If you can't be still and wait, you can't become what God created you to be." [8]

Was that God's purpose in making Abraham and Sarah wait on the promised child? Was God giving them an opportunity to grow into wise and ready parents? We don't know. But wait they do. Not for months, or years, but for decades. Abraham's in his 90s; Sarah in her 80s . . . and still they wait.

Dr. Ray Pritchard gives us a humorous chronology of the 25 years between the time God first promised Abraham and Sarah offspring and the time when the promise was fulfilled:

At age 76, Abraham buys a crib

At age 78, they make a list of possible boy names

At age 80, they order a supply of super-absorbent Pampers

At age 85, Abraham goes hunting while Sarah's friends give her a baby shower.

At age 86, they put up wallpaper in the baby's room

At age 90, they subscribe to *New Parent* magazine

At age 93, Abraham and Sarah start Lamaze classes

At age 96, Abraham drives a practice run to the hospital

At age 98, he packs the suitcase and sets it by the tent door

At age 99, Abraham scratches his head and says, "I wonder if God was just kidding."

God wasn't kidding. Sarah finally gets pregnant. Can you imagine what those nine months were like for Abraham and Sarah? After all their years of heartache, they were finally expecting a child ordained by God. It reminds me of an exchange between two old friends, Bob and John.

"How does Janice like being pregnant?" Bob asked John.

"Oh, she's not pregnant," John replied, "she's expecting."

"What's the difference?" Bob pressed.

"Well," John explained, "She's expecting me to cook dinner, she's expecting me to do the housework, she's expecting me to rub her feet . . ." [10]

At her age, after all she'd been through, Sarah certainly deserved some extra pampering during her pregnancy. When Abraham was 100 and Sarah was 90, she bore a son and they named him Isaac, which means "laughter."

"God has brought me laughter, and everyone who hears about this will laugh with me."

Isaac's birth was an event of great happiness. They finally had a child of their own. And they had seen the promise of God fulfilled. Frederick Buechner once wrote, "The reason Abraham and Sarah laughed was that it suddenly dawned on them that the wildest dreams they'd ever had hadn't been wild enough."

Isaac's birth was truly a miracle. In fact, we might ask whether the birth of Jesus was any more extraordinary than the birth of Isaac— or that of John the Baptist, for that matter. Is it any more difficult for God to use a virgin's womb than that of a woman far past the normal age of child-bearing? Such events are miraculous by any standard.

Sometime back the press reported that a 65-year-old retired schoolteacher in India had become the world's oldest mother when she gave birth to a baby boy. The baby was not conceived naturally, but was the combination of an egg from the woman's 26-year-old niece and the sperm of her husband. The previous record was held by a 63-year-old Italian mother. Before that, the record holder was a 58-year-old woman from Bombay.

Science is already extending the age of child-bearing far beyond its natural boundaries. And, of course, there is the frightening prospect of cloning human embryos.

In light of the continuing wonders that science is producing, it is absurd to deny God the ability to produce miraculous births as well, whether from a 90-year-old woman or from a virgin.

So Abraham and Sarah now have their long-promised child. Again, we'd like to say they lived happily ever after, but their lack of faith earlier in life comes back to haunt them. It's not unusual. Seeds we have sown at one stage in our life often bear fruit at a later stage.

When Abraham and Sarah's beloved son Isaac was about three years old it was time for him to be "weaned." This called for a celebration. However, in the midst of this celebration something unsettling took place. Sarah saw her son Isaac playing with Ishmael, Abraham's other son by the slave woman, Hagar.

The deep resentment and bitterness on Sarah's part that we noted earlier was evidently still festering. The depiction in Scripture is that Abraham had no further interest in Hagar once her role as a surrogate was accomplished. But Sarah could not put the fact out of her mind that Hagar bore Abraham a son. It's easy to empathize with her. Hers was a very human reaction.

Sarah saw Ishmael playing with her son Isaac. She was filled with jealousy and anger. In fact her rage had grown to the point that she wanted Abraham to get rid of this woman and her son. She said to Abraham, "Cast out this slave woman with her son; for the son of this slave woman shall not inherit along with my son, Isaac."

It sounds very much like a television soap opera, doesn't it? *All My Children*? *As the Millstone Turns*? What happens next, though, is unthinkable—even by soap opera standards. Abraham has a decision to make. Ishmael is his son and Hagar is the mother of this son. And yet his wife, Sarah, has ordered him to dispose of the pair of them. What was he to do? At this point God speaks to Abraham.

"Do not be distressed because of the boy and because of your slave woman," God told Abraham. "I will make a nation of him also, because he is your offspring."

And so Abraham makes a mind-boggling decision. He casts Hagar and Ishmael out from the protection of his home. Even worse, he sends them into the desert with only a skin filled with water and a little bit of bread to sustain them. How did he think they would survive?

Let's give Abraham the benefit of the doubt. Let's assume he did this because he really believed God would take care of them. Otherwise, this is one of the great domestic crimes in the history of humanity.

The hot desert was no place for Hagar and Ishmael to be without adequate provisions. Soon their food and water ran out. Hagar could not stand to see her son suffer. With great anguish, she found some shade in the desert and left Ismael there to die. Hagar cried out, "Do not let me look on the death of the child." And she sat down in the desert and began to weep her heart out. Can you imagine a more heart-breaking scene?

God heard Ishmael's cries. Remember the literal meaning of Ishmael's name? "God hears." Thank God for that—literally! Otherwise this is a grim story indeed!

An angel called to Hagar, "What troubles you, Hagar?" Hagar poured out her story. The angel sought to comfort her. "Do not be afraid. Lift up the boy and hold him fast with your hand, for I will make a great nation of him."

As Hagar dried her tears the angel showed her a well where she and her son could draw water. They would not die in the desert. God would be with them. And Ishmael would father a people, too, just as God had promised.

Now, as broadcaster Paul Harvey used to say, "Here is the rest of the story . . ."

There is a group of people in the world today who trace their lineage all the way back to Ishmael. They are, of course, the followers of the prophet Mohammad. The people of Islam. They see themselves as heirs to the promise of God just as the children of Israel, Isaac's son, see themselves as heirs to God's promise. Should we be surprised that the people of Islam want their place in the sun just as you and I want our place in the sun? And regardless of the recklessness and the wanton destructiveness of their extremist elements, the children of Ishmael have a God-given right to that place.

The descendants of Hagar are today's Muslims. In the present moment there are about twelve million Jews in the world, a billion Muslims and two billion Christians. All of us call Abraham "father." Isn't that interesting? All three faiths trace their roots back to this ancient story. The word *Muslim* actually means "one who submits to God." It is a reflection of the faith of Abraham, so highly praised in the New Testament.

While so many of us sympathize with the state of Israel in the current conflicts in the Mid-east, let us not forget that the people of Islam are children of Abraham as well. They also deserve our sympathy. While we can never condone acts of violence against innocent civilians, neither can we ignore the legitimate grievances of this large segment of the world's population.

Would you like to know how the story of Abraham and Sarah ends? It's really quite fascinating. Sarah died at the age of 127, and Abraham mourned for her. He bought a very expensive, special field in which to bury her. Abraham was ten years older than Sarah. When she died, he was 137. He lived 38 more years after her death.

Abraham remarried after Sarah's death, which is pretty remarkable for a 137-year-old man. Abraham died at age 175. And he was buried beside his beloved Sarah. He left all his inheritance to his son, Isaac. And yet, guess who was there for Abraham's burial? His banished son Ishmael. Ishmael helped Isaac bury their father.

Interestingly, in the biblical record, Ishmael showed no sign of resentment over his treatment by his father. Neither did he show resentment over the fact that Isaac inherited all of Abraham's considerable wealth. However, the twenty-fifth chapter of Genesis contains a dramatic footnote to our story. It says that Ishmael's descendants settled near the border of Egypt. And listen to these words from the eighteenth verse: "And they lived in hostility toward all their brothers . . ." This, of course, was just as the angel had earlier predicted.

Hmm. Could it be that we are still paying for a father's mistreatment of his son more than 3,000 years ago? Could we be paying for Abraham's and Sarah's unwillingness to trust God and their use of a slave girl to fulfill their own desires?

On March 26, 1979 an Egyptian–Israeli peace treaty was signed by Egyptian President Anwar Sadat and Israeli Prime Minister Menachem Begin in Washington, DC, following the Camp David Accords, a series of meetings between Egypt and Israel facilitated by President Jimmy Carter. Both Sadat and Begin were awarded the Nobel Peace Prize for creating the treaty. In his acceptance speech, Sadat spoke of the need to reconcile the sons of Ishmael with those of Isaac, a need that continues to this day.

Why are these old, old stories from the Bible important to us? Because they are still being lived out today. Problems of trust. Stress within families. Sins of the father visited on the children. And one saving grace—faith. Faith in one another. Faith in God.

Abraham and Sarah were not perfect people. But they had faith in a perfect God—and they had faith in each other. With God's help they made it through.

ISAAC AND REBEKAH

Genesis 24:34-38, 42-49, 58-67

Comedians have a field day with the subject of marriage. The jokes probably number in the thousands.

Rita Rudner used this classic: "My mother buried three husbands . . . And two of them were just napping."

One woman said to a friend: "I'm in trouble. I broke my husband's favorite golf club."

"What did he say?" her friend asked.

The first woman smiled and replied, "He said, 'What hit me?'"

The late Erma Bombeck had this to say: "People are always asking couples whose marriages have endured at least a quarter of a century for their secret for success. Actually, it is no secret at all. I am a forgiving woman. Long ago, I forgave my husband for not being Paul Newman."

One anonymous soul, a man, claims, "I married Miss Right. I just didn't know her first name was Always."

And do you think it's just a coincidence, as one man noted, that June, the month of marriages, is followed by July, the month of fireworks?

Few of the marriages in the Bible had as many fireworks as that of Isaac and Rebekah. But before we get into the details of their marriage, we need to probe the life history of Isaac. Maybe there we can get some clues into why he was not a candidate for the Husband-of-the-Year award.

You may remember a few years back when a man was nominated for the Supreme Court of the United States who was so lacking in accomplishments that one of his supporters defended him by saying that "mediocre people deserved a representative on the Supreme Court, too."

Mediocre people have many representatives in Scripture, but none who exceed the mediocrity of Isaac. That's cruel to say. God still chose to use Isaac for his eternal purposes. But to hear Isaac's name mentioned in the exalted description of the eternal God—"The God of Abraham, the God of Isaac, the God of Jacob"—seems rather incongruous.

We find Isaac sandwiched between two giants of Scripture, his father Abraham and his son Jacob. We expect more out of Isaac than he shows us in these chapters in Genesis. Isaac was not a giant of Scripture. He was a man of modest abilities and faith.

In the stories we remember best about him, he is a minor character. We've already noted how he received his name. His mother laughed when she was told that she would bear a son in her old age. Thus Abraham and Sarah named their new born son, Isaac, or "Laughter."

Names can make a difference in a child's life. Perhaps they should have named him Rocky. Laughter is such a soft, non-threatening name. I have often thought, however, that it would give us a different image of the God of the Old Testament if we read this description of God, —"The God of Abraham, the God of Laughter, the God of Jacob . . . ." Personally, I like the idea that God is the God of Laughter.

Laughter's father, or I should say, Isaac's father was 100; his mother, 90, when he was born. Maybe this is why he did not develop the presence or the stature he needed to impose his name on history. Many outstanding people have had older parents, but not as old as Isaac's.

Maybe at this stage in life Abraham and Sarah were not very adept at parenting. Maybe they nodded off during Isaac's piano recitals. Instead of bedtime stories, maybe they read him articles out of *AARP* magazine. Could it be that Sarah's failing eyesight caused her to switch her arthritis cream for Isaac's baby lotion?

Or perhaps, after seeing Sarah banish Isaac's half-brother Ishmael and his mother Hagar into the wilderness, neighborhood moms were reluctant to send their kids over to play with Isaac.

Perhaps it was that traumatic episode in the wilderness a little later in Isaac's life. You know the one I'm thinking of. Isaac was twelve years old. The Scripture begins the story with these ominous words: "Some time later God tested Abraham . . ." (Gen. 22:1).

And here was the dreaded test: God said, "Take your son, your only son, Isaac, whom you love, and go to the region of Moriah. Sacrifice him there as a burnt offering on one of the mountains I will tell you about."

Sometimes, when we sense that God is calling us to do something difficult, we are tempted to protest, "But God doesn't know what He's asking. That can't possibly be God's will. Doesn't God know how much that would hurt?" Let it sink in: "Take your son, your only son, Isaac, **whom you love,** and go to the region of Moriah. Sacrifice him there as a burnt offering . . ." This passage shows us that God knows full well just how much this command will hurt Abraham.

It is difficult for us to reconcile the image of God in this story to the image of God we see in the teachings of Jesus. Sacrifice your son as a burnt offering? Sounds more like a primitive pagan god than *Abba,* "Daddy."

You've heard the classic joke, no doubt: Why did God have Abraham go to the sacrificial mountain to test him by asking his to sacrifice his only son, Isaac, when Isaac was only 12? Because, if Isaac had been 15, Abraham may have actually gone through with it. Just kidding, of course.

God knew how much Abraham loved his son. What God had commanded Abraham to do was thus unthinkable, even unbelievable. No sane parent would willingly harm his or her child. It was an outrageous request. Maybe Abraham should have his hearing checked. Maybe he didn't hear everything God told him. Isaac was the child of promise. Isaac was Abraham's link to the future. What about that promise God made to Abraham that he would father a great nation? What happens to that promise if Isaac is no longer around? The whole request seemed so inconceivable, so outrageous, so unfair. How would he tell Sarah that he would offer their only son as a sacrifice?

This is a difficult passage in Scripture for many Christians to reconcile with their understanding of Jesus. Exodus 20:20 tells us that God tests us to confirm our faith or to prove our commitment. Or, as someone once wrote, "Satan tempts us to bring out the worst in us; God tests us to bring out the best in us." [11]

God tested Abraham. And how does Abraham respond? Our Bible verse reads, "Early the next morning Abraham got up and saddled his donkey." Early the next morning. We could understand if he had slept in a few extra hours. Any man in his position might hesitate for a while. But not Abraham. No matter how much it hurt, he would be obedient to God.

Andrew Young, former Ambassador to the UN, was talking about his daughter's decision to work in a very dangerous part of Africa. Young said something like this, "When we brought her to church and Sunday school, when we had her baptized, we didn't really know that she was going to take all of this religion so seriously! It's sort of scary to realize that you are putting your own child at risk when you bring her to the Lord!" [12]

Isaac's life had been consecrated to the Lord. He belonged to God. There was no turning back. Abraham and Isaac traveled for three days to reach Mount Moriah, the place of the sacrifice.

For three days, Abraham had time to think about losing his son. What memories haunted him over those three days? Did he remember the day of God's promise to him? Did he remember Isaac's first word, his first smile, his first step?

At the foot of the mountain, Abraham left his servants behind with the donkey. He and Isaac were going up the mountain to worship. And then Abraham says something interesting: "We will come back to you." "**We** will come back to you." Was this a lie? Wishful thinking? Or a breathtaking declaration of faith in the God he had followed for so long?

Abraham laid the wood for the sacrifice on Isaac's back. As they trudged up the mountain, Isaac asked where the lamb was for the offering. Abraham replied, "God himself will provide the lamb for the burnt offering, my son."

At the top of the mountain, Abraham built an altar. Then, he tied up Isaac and placed him on the wood. Abraham raised the knife, ready to strike, when a voice from heaven cried out, "Abraham! Abraham! Do not lay a hand on the boy. Do not do anything to him.

Now I know that you fear God, because you have not withheld from me your son, your only son."

When Abraham looked up, he saw a ram caught in a nearby thicket. He removed Isaac from the altar and sacrificed the ram instead. And from that day on, Abraham called that place *The Lord Will Provide*.

We may be shocked by this story. We may question the existence of a good and loving God when we hear this story. But notice that the person who was asked to make this radical commitment, Abraham, never questioned God's motives. He never questioned God's goodness. The man at the heart of the matter trusted God completely.

I said that this is a difficult passage in Scripture for many Christians to reconcile with their understanding of Jesus. And yet the story is repeated at the end of Jesus' life on Calvary. This time, however, it is God who makes the sacrifice. In the beautiful language of Scripture, God again provides a lamb for the sacrifice. However, the Lamb is his own Son.

We don't know what kind of effect this experience might have had on Isaac. If the story is shocking for us to read, imagine what it must have been for him to experience.

In the next major milestone in Isaac's life, he is a passive observer again. Only this time he is an adult, and his father is choosing a bride for him.

Like many cultures in ancient times the Hebrews practiced arranged marriages. Actually this practice may appeal to many parents today. The choice of a life-long mate seems too serious to leave to teenagers. Even more important, young people in love are selecting the father or the mother of their parents' potential grandchildren. Much is at stake.

Whether our current system of young people falling in love works better than the old system of arranged marriages is yet to be determined. The old marriages seemed to last a lot longer.

Abraham selected a trusted servant and sent him back to his own people to find a wife for Isaac. So, Isaac is still living at home. He is a precursor of many of today's young men who finish school and then move back in with Mom and Dad. Of course, for our current generation of young people, this is often because of economic necessity.

Abraham instructed the servant that the selected bride must not be a Canaanite nor from any of the other pagan peoples in the region. To encourage the servant, Abraham promised him that an angel of the Lord would guide him in this endeavor. If he chose a potential bride, however, and she refused to come, the servant was freed from his responsibility.

Let's pick up the story now in detail. The servant has gone back to Abraham's ancestral home. He's waiting near a spring where maidens would come to draw water. And he lays claim on God's help. "O Lord," he prays in his heart, "God of my master Abraham, if you will, please grant success to the journey on which I have come. See, I am standing beside this spring; if a maiden comes out to draw water and I say to her, 'Please let me drink a little water from your jar,' and if she says to me, 'Drink, and I'll draw water for your camels too,' let her be the one the Lord has chosen for my master's son."

Then something dramatic happened. Before the servant had even finished praying, a young beauty named Rebekah came out with her jar on her shoulder. She went down to the spring and drew water. The servant approached her cautiously and said, "Please give me a drink."

And Rebekah quickly lowered her jar from her shoulder and said, "Drink, and I'll water your camels too." So the servant drank while Rebekah watered the camels.

This Hebrew maiden was passing the test with flying colors. And it's a pretty good test of character, if you think about it. Rebekah showed compassion for the servant and for his animal as well. The servant immediately believed he had found the perfect bride for Isaac. He asked her, "Whose daughter are you?" And much to his delight he discovered she was from exactly the right family.

Now listen to these interesting words. They are the words of the servant: "Then I put the ring in her nose and the bracelets on her arms, and I bowed down and worshiped the Lord. I praised the Lord, the God of my master Abraham, who had led me on the right road."

"I put the ring in her nose . . ." Do you think that pierced body parts are something new? There is nothing new under the sun. By the way, I hope this doesn't affect the image that you may have of Isaac and Rebekah. I know it is difficult for me to imagine Bible heroes with rings in their noses.

The servant knew he had found the right girl for his master's son. Now he must get the approval of Rebekah's family. He found them to be quite cordial to his inquiry. They had only one condition that we know of. They wanted to make sure this was something that Rebekah wanted. After all, she had never laid eyes on her potential husband. And it would mean leaving home and traveling to a distant land.

They called Rebekah and asked her, "Will you go with this man?"

"I will go," she said. That was it. Obviously Rebekah was ready. "I will go." This was the moment she had been waiting for a long time. Hot dog! So they sent Rebekah on her way, along with her nurse and Abraham's servant and his men.

Now, what about Isaac's reaction to the young woman who was to be his bride?

Isaac was out in a field meditating when he saw camels approaching. Rebekah also looked up and saw Isaac. She got down from her camel and asked the servant, "Who is that man in the field coming to meet us?"

"He is my master," the servant answered. So she took her veil and covered herself.

Then the servant told Isaac the story of how he went about selecting Rebekah. The writer of Genesis says, "Isaac brought her into the tent of his mother Sarah, and he married Rebekah. So she became his wife, and he loved her; and Isaac was comforted after his mother's death."

That's interesting, isn't it? "Isaac was comforted after his mother's death." Cynically we might think, poor old mediocre Isaac just needed a replacement for his mother. Again, it's not fair, but stay with us. Isaac doesn't inspire much confidence in the stories yet to come either.

On a more positive note, we see here the cycle of life lived out. A man and woman go out from their homes and pledge themselves to one another. They still love their parents, but they make a new life for themselves. This is one of the things that will make it bearable for them when they lose a parent to death. Now they have one another.

I would like to say Isaac and Rebekah lived happily ever after, but that would not be true. It would not even be close to true.

A little girl had just been told the story of "Snow White" for the first time. She could hardly wait to get home from nursery school to tell her mommy. With wide-eyed excitement, she retold the fairy tale to her mother that afternoon. After relating how Prince Charming had arrived on his beautiful white horse and kissed Snow White back to life, the little girl asked loudly: "And do you know what happened then?"

"Yes," said her mom, "they lived happily ever after."

"No," responded the little girl with a frown, "They got married."

Married life is difficult under the best of conditions. The melding of two personalities is never easy.

Ed Young tells about a spot in North Carolina where two rivers come together. "There is a bluff high above the place where you can see them moving placidly and calmly toward their meeting point, but where they converge a battle is going on. One strong, smooth, independent stream meets an equally strong, smooth, independent stream—and the water from both churns and splashes and foams in a noisy, rushing current. From the vantage point of the bluff," says Ed Young, "it is obvious that after their somewhat violent meeting, these two bodies of water combine to form a wider, more impressive river than either was originally." [13]

Isaac and Rebekah never achieved that kind of synthesis. Their marriage was more like the churning, splashing, rushing current than it was a placid river.

For example, we read that in the kingdom of Abimelech Isaac repeats the sin of his father, Abraham, in passing off Rebekah as his sister out of fear for his own well-being. Like father, like son.

Perhaps these stories are too much alike. It might help us if we understood that these stories in the first books of the Bible were passed down orally for many generations before they were written down. Imagine a wandering family of Hebrews happening upon the fallen ruins of an ancient Babylonian ziggurat in the desert. That night around the campfire the father might tell his son the story that his father before him had told that once upon a time the peoples of the world tried to build a great tower that would reach into the heavens that they might make a name for themselves. Thus the story of the fall of the tower of Babel would be preserved.

But, telling these stories from memory, it would not be unusual if the story teller included details from one story in the telling of another. It may have happened with the stories of Abraham and Isaac. For our purposes, however, we will take the text at face value, that Isaac passed off Rebekah as his sister out of fear.

There is one good thing to say about Isaac—he was a good provider. In fact, Isaac and Rebekah became very wealthy. This brought them into conflict with their neighbors. The Philistines came to envy Isaac's prosperity. As an act of spite they began to fill in all of Isaac's wells. Isaac and Rebekah became so wealthy that even King Abimelech felt threatened. He asked Isaac and Rebekah to move on, which they did.

God kept His promises to Isaac, just as he had with his father, Abraham. God kept His promises not because of who Isaac was, but because of who God is. This is a story of grace. God is faithful even when human beings are not.

The most important event in the lives of Isaac and Rebekah was, of course, the birth of their two sons. For a time Rebekah was barren, but Isaac prayed for God's help and she became pregnant with twins. Twin boys. Be careful what you pray for.

Rebekah had a horrible pregnancy. So she went to inquire of the Lord. The Lord said to her, "Two nations are in your womb, and two peoples from within you will be separated; one people will be stronger than the other, and the older will serve the younger."

So, Rebekah knew something that Isaac did not: of the two, the younger boy carried the promise of God. Perhaps that is the reason Rebekah would favor Jacob, the younger of the two brothers.

The Lord told Rebekah that the two children which she carried in her womb would struggle against one another. And they did. Even before the twins were born, they were at odds. When they emerged from the womb, the younger son whom they named Jacob (which means "holding to his heel") was holding on to the heel of the older boy, Esau (which means "red and hairy"), trying to be born first.

That was an omen. The two boys were constantly trying to outdo one another. You know the time-honored stories. Esau sold his birthright to Jacob for a bowl of stew. Jacob tricked their aging father into giving him the blessing which rightfully belonged to Esau. Esau was naturally irate. Jacob subsequently fled to his uncle Laban's home out of fear for his life.

The real tragedy in the story, however, is that Mom and Dad took sides. Isaac preferred the manly, outdoor-oriented Esau. Rebekah felt protective toward the gentler, shrewder Jacob. Before long a serious rift developed in the family—a rift that was devastating. The last time we see Rebekah, she is sending Jacob far off to live with her brother Laban while she remains to stand up to Isaac and Esau. As for Esau, Genesis 26 tells us that when Esau was forty years old, he married two Hittite women (which was a no-no). The writer of Genesis reports, "They were a source of grief to Isaac and Rebekah."

Isaac was not the towering figure in the Scriptures that his father had been. Probably he did not command Rebekah's respect. The tension between them manifested itself in the raising of the twins.

You have to wonder, though, if the rift was really over the boys at all. Maybe it grew out of a lack of intimacy between the parents, parents acting out their own problems by pitting their sons against one another.

Perhaps in her desire to fool her husband into blessing Jacob instead of Esau, Rebakah was not acting out of her own selfish desires at all. Maybe she was simply more sensitive spiritually to God's leading in this matter. God had told her that the older would serve the younger. Certainly, Jacob was a more worthy leader of the Jews than Esau could ever have been.

Whatever the root cause, this was not a happy home. They were wealthy, secure. God prospered Isaac as God promised. The boys were healthy and they both did all right for themselves. But it was not until they were old men that the twins, Jacob and Esau, restored the bond that was their birthright. We'll pick up that story in the next chapter.

That happens in life, doesn't it? It takes a real commitment to make a marriage work, any marriage. It takes a willingness to yield to another's desire. It takes a common dream. It takes parents who do not use their children as pawns in their own marital conflicts.

The best that can be said for Isaac and Rebekah is that they survived. When they died, they were buried beside Abraham and Sarah.

Mediocre people with a mediocre marriage. They could have done much better—and so can we. But it takes a real determination. All of us who live East of Eden struggle to create intimacy. We struggle to overcome our innate need to dominate others, to put our own needs first. We struggle with creating oneness while maintaining our own identity. We continually hurt the ones we love the most. Though they lived thousands of years ago in a culture radically different from our own, Isaac and Rebekah could be our neighbors. They could be us.

An assistant professor of family relations and child development at Oklahoma State University was trying to figure out what makes couples stay together. Linda Robinson searched out 15 couples who had been married 35 years or longer in order to study the secrets of marital success. It is significant that most of the people she interviewed were churchgoers, had at least one child, and were highly educated.

After the interviews, Robinson synthesized all her information into a list of characteristics that can be found in a lasting marriage: commitment to the institution of marriage, commitment to one's spouse, communication, autonomy, religious faith, willingness to compromise on issues.

There were other important characteristics that were not mentioned as much, but the one characteristic that transcended all others was intimacy, time for communication and "connectedness" with one's spouse. [14]

Isaac and Rebekah wouldn't have scored well in any of these areas, but notice this: In spite of Isaac and Rebekah's shortcomings, God still used them to continue God's work on earth. That should give us hope. In spite of their bumbling efforts, their sons Jacob and Esau eventually turned out to be fine men—men whom God blessed in a real way. And that's our hope. If we live responsibly and stay faithful to God's call, God will watch over us and keep us in the ways we would go.

JACOB AND RACHEL
Genesis 28-35

One more joke about marriage: A man was sitting at the bar in his local tavern, furiously imbibing shots of whiskey. One of his friends happens to come into the bar and sees him.

"Lou," says the shocked friend, "what are you doing? I've known you for over fifteen years, and I've never seen you take a drink before. What's going on?"

Without even taking his eyes off his shot glass, Lou replies, "My wife just ran off with my best friend." He then throws back another shot of whiskey in one gulp.

"But," says the other man, "I'M your best friend!"

Lou turns to his friend, looks at him through bloodshot eyes, smiles, and slurs, "Not anymore!" [15]

Men like to make jokes about marriage. And yet, most men prefer married life. That's what studies show. In fact, studies show that men are happier in their marriages than are their wives.

Civil rights activist Andrew Young was married to his wife for forty years before she died. After her death, Young's friends set him up with many beautiful, accomplished women.

In an interview, Young admits that he was no good at dating. He re-married soon after his wife's death because, as he said, "I needed a relationship of trust and permanence . . . I'm not cut out to be a playboy." [16]

That's true of most men, whether they admit it or not. It was certainly true of the Old Testament patriarch Jacob. He was a scoundrel and a cheat as a young man, but as he matured, he became a man of character who knew how to commit himself to a relationship.

We have already seen how Jacob cheated his brother out of his birthright and then had to flee his brother's wrath. Now he was on his way to Haran—the home of his uncle Laban. It was while Jacob was trying to escape from his brother's wrath that he encountered God.

Jacob "came to a certain place and stayed there for the night." There is an ancient legend that Jacob was so afraid and uncomfortable camping outside that he found rocks and built a wall to protect himself. After all, it was his brother, Esau, who was the outdoor type. Jacob would have been more comfortable at the Holiday Inn. But he was also a fugitive running away. He was uncertain what would happen next. He found a stone and used it for a pillow. Then he fell asleep under the stars.

At that unexpected time and in that unexpected place, God broke into Jacob's world in a dream. Verse 12 of Genesis 28 reads: "He had a dream in which he saw a stairway resting on the earth, with its top reaching to heaven, and the angels of God were ascending and descending on it." The Lord stood above the ladder and declared to Jacob, "I am the Lord, the God of your father Abraham and the God of Isaac. I will give you and your descendants the land on which you are lying. Your descendants will be like the dust of the earth, and you will spread out to the west and to the east, to the north and to the south. All peoples on earth will be blessed through you and your offspring. I am with you and will watch over you wherever you go, and I will bring you back to this land. I will not leave until I have done what I have promised you."

"When Jacob awoke, he thought, 'Surely the Lord is in this place, and I was not aware of it.' He was afraid and said, 'How awesome is this place! This is none other than the house of God; this is the gate of heaven.'"

Here, in a dream, Jacob received the vision for his life, and it was grander than he could have ever imagined. He was scared and grateful and awe-struck all at once, and he did the only thing he knew to do for such a momentous occasion: he built a pillar to mark the spot. And Jacob named this place Bethel, or house of God.

This dream marked a turning point for Jacob the striver, the supplanter. He still is a deal-maker—even with God. As this chapter in Jacob's life closes, he makes a vow, "**If** God will be with me and will watch over me on this journey I am taking and will give me food to eat and clothes to wear so that I return safely to my father's house, **then** the Lord will be my God . . ." (emphasis added).

This is not the unconditional obedience that his grandfather Abraham had demonstrated, but for Jacob it is a major step in his spiritual life. This vision at Bethel marked a new understanding for Jacob of who he was and what was expected of him. Until now, he had used aggression and deception to steal away his brother's blessings. But God was showing Jacob that if he were to be truly blessed, it would not be through his own striving. Instead, Jacob's blessings would come through honoring and following the God of his fathers. He would still be ambitious—but he would be ambitious for pleasing God.

Unfortunately, when Jacob finally becomes a man who no longer cheats to get what he wants, he runs into a man who has no such scruples. It's his uncle Laban. But we're getting ahead of our story.

It's interesting, isn't it? God called Abram (Abraham) to leave his home in Haran to go out and found a new people. But when Jacob, the one heir to Abram who carries in his loins the promise God made to Abram that he would father a great people, leaves his family home, he flees back to Haran. But there is a purpose to the plan. He is to find a wife there who will be of his own people.

This is very important. The brother who stayed home with Mom and Dad, Esau, did not honor his birthright. He married women who were outside his faith. They made life bitter for Isaac and Rebekah, as we have already noted. Jacob the striver, though his life got off to a rocky start, actually lives his life much closer to the family's hopes and dreams, for he married within the desires of his mother and father.

Now he's headed toward the ancestral territory of Haran. Nearly to his destination, he comes upon a well with three flocks of sheep lying nearby preparing to drink. Jacob asks the shepherds, "Where are you from?"

"We're from Haran," they reply.

Excitedly Jacob asks, "Do you know Laban, Nahor's

grandson?"

"Yes, we know him," they answered.

Then Jacob asks them, "Is he well?"

"Yes, he is," they said, "and here comes his daughter Rachel with the sheep."

Jacob's heart does a flip-flop. It doesn't say that in the Scripture, but that is what happened. Rachel, a shepherdess, wandered by with her sheep, and Jacob's heart did a flip-flop. He immediately rushed over and removed the large stone for her that covered the opening to the well. Then, says the Scripture, "Jacob kissed Rachel and began to weep aloud." He told Rachel that he was the son of Rebekah—her father's sister. In a very real sense, he was her "kissing cousin." Then Rachel ran and told her father.

At this point, Jacob's tricky Uncle Laban enters the picture. Laban would never have admitted to being a liar and a cheat. He was simply a shrewd businessman—a man who got the best of every deal.

Two men were discussing the character of a third. "Let me describe him this way," said the first. "He's the kind of guy who follows you into a revolving door and comes out ahead of you." [17] That's Laban in a nutshell.

Laban comes to greet Jacob. He gives him a warm embrace and takes him to his home. There, in the comfort of Laban's home, Jacob spills out all that has happened to him to this point. And Laban takes on Jacob as a hired hand. After the first month, he even asks Jacob what he would like to be paid. Obviously Laban has come to see that Jacob is a bright, young employee who could be a big asset to the family business.

Now the plot begins to thicken. Laban has two daughters; the name of the older daughter is Leah, and the name of the younger daughter is Rachel. Jacob was already in love with Rachel. According to Scripture, "Rachel was lovely in form, and beautiful."

Jacob said, "I'll work for you seven years in return for your younger daughter Rachel." And Laban agreed. Why wouldn't he? What a deal—the services of a bright young employee for seven years in return for marrying off one of his daughters.

So Jacob served his uncle Laban seven years to get Rachel, but "they seemed like only a few days to him because of his love for her," says the writer of Genesis. Isn't young love wonderful?

After the seven years, Jacob asks Laban to fulfill his end of the bargain and let him have Rachel as his wife. So a wedding feast is held and Jacob retires to the bridal chamber with his new bride. But the next morning he awakes to discover that he is not married to Rachel at all, but to her plainer older sister, Leah.

Jacob rushed directly to Laban, "What have you done to me?" he asked angrily. "I served you for Rachel—not Leah."

And Laban coolly replied, "It is not our custom here to give the younger daughter in marriage before the older one. Marrying Rachel will cost you another seven years."

And Jacob agreed! Talk about being smitten. Jacob had it bad. And he worked for Laban another seven years.

This is love beyond all reasonable bounds. Fourteen years of labor, just to win the fair maiden's hand. But through it all, we see how different Jacob is from his pre-Bethel days. He has become a man of principle, a man of character.

That's the kind of man you want to love you if you are a woman, isn't it—a man of principle and character? A man you can depend on? Jacob is now that kind of man.

After all this, we would like to say that Jacob and Rachel lived happily ever after. But, don't forget, there were two wives in the household. In fantasy, that may appeal to some men; in reality, it is a recipe for disaster. Jacob was saddled with Rachel AND Leah. It did not matter that Jacob loved Rachel more than Leah. In fact, that fact led to much intrigue. A contest began for Jacob's affection.

Leah began bearing children. The writer of Genesis says this was to compensate Leah for the fact that Jacob was partial to Rachel. Rachel was barren. We have already seen an example of the anguish these Old Testament women experienced when they could not bear children.

In all, Leah had six sons and one daughter and she probably lorded this fact over Rachel. In fact, the interaction between the two wives of Jacob would probably make good material for *Desperate Housewives*.

There is a somewhat humorous and earthy scene behind the birth of one of Leah's sons. Reuben, Leah's oldest son, has harvested some mandrake plants (thought, because of their shape, to have both aphrodisiac and fertility qualities).

Rachel said to Leah, "Please give me some of your son's mandrakes."

Leah replied, "Wasn't it enough that you took away my husband? Will you take my son's mandrakes too?"

"Very well," Rachel said, "[Jacob] can sleep with you tonight in return for your son's mandrakes."

So when Jacob came in from the fields that evening, Leah went out to meet him. "You must sleep with me," she said. "I have hired you with my son's mandrakes." So Jacob slept with her that night. And Leah, of course, became pregnant and bore Jacob yet another son.

I believe that is called irony. Rachel made the deal for the mandrakes in the desperate hope that she would become pregnant, and who has another son? Leah. She called him Assachar.

Later, another son arrived for Leah, called Zebulun. Finally, she bore Jacob a daughter, Dinah.

In order that she might give her husband children, the distraught Rachel gave Jacob her maid, Bilhah, to have children. Bilhah bore Jacob two sons. So, to keep things even, Leah's maid bore Jacob two sons. Jacob is probably nearing exhaustion by this point.

Finally, Rachel bore Jacob a son, Joseph. That's Joseph, as in "the coat of many colors" which, of course sets up another episode of intrigue in the Old Testament narrative. You would think that Jacob would have learned from his father's and mother's mistakes about playing favorites. But later, in chapter 37, we read these ominous words: "Now Israel (Jacob) loved Joseph more than any of his other sons . . . When his brothers saw that their father loved him more than any of them, they hated him and could not speak a kind word to him."

But we are getting ahead of our story. It will not serve our purpose here to include all of the shenanigans that take place next. Laban is still trying to take advantage of Jacob, but God intervenes and gives Jacob the victory. Finally Jacob flees the land taking his family, flocks and possessions.

Now it is time for Jacob to head home to Canaan. He had some unfinished business there with his brother Esau. Jacob was ready to confront this relationship. Little did he know that on his way to meet his brother, Jacob would also confront some unfinished business with God. This business is taken care of at a place which he would later call Peniel (which means "face of God.")

Jacob camped by a brook, and there Jacob wrestled all night long with God. You'll remember that at Bethel Jacob had prayed a conditional prayer, "**If** God will be with me, and keep me in this way that I go, and will give me bread to eat, and raiment to put on, so that I come again to my father's house in peace; **then** the Lord shall be my God." (Gen. 28: 20) However, Jacob prayed a different prayer as he prepared to bed down beside the brook. He prayed this time, "O God . . . I am not worthy of the least of all thy mercies . . ."

Something profound was happening in Jacob's life, and it was more than fear of his brother. It had to do with the recognition of who God is and who we as human beings are. Jacob wrestled with God.

Jacob had always been a competitor, a striver, with man and with God. He knew what he wanted. He was determined to control his own destiny. He would master the possibilities. The sky was the limit. Do you know anyone like that? They have always been with us—men and women determined to grab all the gusto that life has to offer them, and when they do, they discover themselves holding a handful of foam—nothing real or lasting.

Jacob needed something more. He needed an overall purpose for his life. He needed to understand where his life fit into the overall scheme of things. Suddenly he saw that his life was nearly over and all that he had thought was important would soon be dust. "What does it all mean? Who am I, really? Does my life really matter?"

As he wrestled with God that night, the encounter was so demanding that he threw the hollow of his thigh out of joint. One thinks of Jesus kneeling in the garden of Gethsemane with drops of sweat like great drops of blood falling from his brow. This was that kind of encounter for Jacob. He was engaged in a spiritual struggle that required every ounce of his strength. From this day forward, he would never be the same again.

For you see, Jacob needed more than anything else in life to understand that God was the Master of the universe and not Jacob. It is interesting that the being with whom Jacob wrestles does not prevail over him. Jacob is like a grand stallion. It is not God's desire that Jacob grovel at his feet. God has no use for one who is continually groveling. God wanted a grand stallion, but one who could be useful, one who could be saddled, one who would know who his Master is that he might fulfill his intended purpose. [18] That is what God desires from us, as well. Our lives are useful only to ourselves and only for a season if we refuse to give God the reins.

Jacob wrestles with God and God gives him a new name. The name is Israel which means, "you have struggled with God and with men and have overcome."

The writer of Genesis closes this chapter in Jacob's life with a beautiful picture. It is a picture of a limping Jacob preparing to meet his brother Esau. He is no longer afraid of Esau. After all, he has wrestled all night with God. How can he fear a mere mortal? But now he is a new Jacob. He even has a new name, Israel. He will become a prince among men. Forevermore his descendants, millions of them, will be known as the children of Israel. As the sun rises over Peniel we see him standing there with a dislocated thigh. He is a broken man, yet he is stronger than he has ever been before. His life is now aligned with the eternal purposes of God.

There is a story about a man who had misspent most of his life. A friend was teasing him about it. "Say John," he asked mischievously, "You still spending a lot of time wrestling with the old Devil?"

The fellow answered good-naturedly, "Nowadays, I spend most of my time wrestling with God."

His friend asked incredulously, "Wrestling with God? How do you hope to win a wrestling match with God?"

John smiled and answered, "Oh, you misunderstand. In this wrestling match, I'm hoping to lose."

We can see the new humble Jacob in his encounter with his brother Esau. Jacob expects Esau to hold a grudge. What he does not expect is for his brother to forgive him. Imagine Jacob's surprise when Esau runs to meet him and catches him up in a hug.

At Peniel, Jacob experiences grace—an undeserved blessing—from God and from his brother. Grace has the power to humble us even today, to break our hearts wide open with the unexpected power of undeserved love. Jacob presents Esau with a gift which Esau seeks to refuse. And Jacob says, "No, please! If I have found favor in your eyes, accept this gift from me. For to see your face is like seeing the face of God, now that you have received me favorably. Please accept the present that was brought to you, for God has been gracious to me and I have all I need." And because Jacob insisted, Esau accepted it.

So Jacob returned to Canaan. He now has a new name, Israel.

He has eleven sons (six by Leah, four by servant girls and one, Joseph, by Rachel). Finally Rachel becomes pregnant again, and she bears him a son, Benjamin. Sadly, Jacob's beloved Rachel dies while giving birth to Benjamin. Another sad irony in Rachel's life. She prayed to God, "Give me children or I shall die!" (30:1) And she died in childbirth.

Jacob buries her in Bethlehem (it's interesting how often Bethlehem turns up in these ancient love stories).

In spite of the historical oddities in this story—such as the cultural practice of having multiple wives and using slave girls as surrogates—the story of Jacob and Rachel is one of history's great love stories. It is a story of commitment and principle. It is a reminder to us that great love can exist—even in our modern world.

I read a story recently that reminded me of the reality of such love.

Buckminster Fuller or "Bucky," as he was known to his friends, was a legendary architect. He had one of the most imaginative minds of the twentieth century. Among his creations was the geodesic dome.

Buckminster Fuller had always promised his beloved wife, Annie, that he would die before she did. He said that he wanted to be in Heaven to welcome her when she arrived. But in their later years, Annie became very ill. Fuller, though elderly, was in good health. It looked as though he might have to break his promise.

One day, Annie slipped into a coma. Doctors speculated that she would never recover. As Buckminster Fuller sat by his wife's bedside, he simply closed his eyes and died. Just like that. It was as if he had willed himself to die first. A few hours later, Annie died too. They had gotten their wish. Fuller was there to welcome his wife to Heaven. [19]

That was the intense kind of love Jacob had for Rachel. It's the kind of love about which books are written and poems composed.

But perhaps you like to cheer for the underdog. Perhaps you feel a great empathy for Leah, the homely one, the "other wife."

There's no question that Jacob preferred Rachel and resented being married to Leah. A good example is found in Genesis 32-33. When Jacob was about to meet his brother Esau for the first time since their bitter parting, Jacob expected that Esau would attack with his 400 men, so he put Leah and her children near the front of the line, and kept Rachel and her child safely in the rear. That had to be both terrifying and humiliating for Leah.

Leah's pain is very real from the very beginning of this ill-conceived marriage. We can see this in the names she chose for her sons. According to Gen. 29:32-34, she named her firstborn, Reuben, because "the Lord has seen my misery." She named her second son, Simeon, because "the Lord heard that I am not loved." And when her third son was born, she named him, Levi, saying "Now at last my husband will become attached to me."

How very sad—to always be number two in her husband's affections.

It might cheer you to know, however, that somewhere along the way, after Rachel's death Jacob and Leah bonded. When Jacob dies as an old man, he is buried not beside Rachel, but beside Leah. Love the second time around is not a betrayal of that first love. It simply signifies a change of life situation.

It's interesting. The Lord had promised Jacob that he would have many descendants (28.14), but Jacob's beloved wife Rachel, died giving birth to her second son. Had Jacob had things his way with regard to Rachel and Leah, God's promise would not have been fulfilled.

Here's what's really interesting, though. We usually focus on Rachel's older son Joseph and what he meant in the story of Abraham's descendants. But note what happened to two of Leah's sons. The line of her third son Levi produced Israel's priesthood (the Levites). Notably in this line you find Moses, Aaron, Elizabeth, and John the Baptist.

Leah's fourth son, Judah, was the ancestor of the house of David, the kingly family, including "Joseph, the husband of Mary, of whom was born Jesus who is called Christ." That's right. The Messiah was born of Leah's offspring, not Rachel's.

Love and marriage. Principle and character. These are people we can all relate to. And in the shadows is a loving God who is working out His plan for creation. God had made a promise to Jacob's grandfather, Abraham, that he would father a great people. God's dreams for His people were carried through Jacob the striver, who had his life turned around at a place called Peniel. May we who are God's children today find our Peniel too.

Jacob's twelve sons later become the twelve tribes of Israel.

Many years later, when Jacob is old and feeble and facing his own death, he would leave a blessing for his own grandsons, the children of Jacob's favorite son, Joseph. And this was the blessing that he gave: "May the God before whom my fathers Abraham and Isaac walked, the God who has been my shepherd all my life to this day, the Angel who has delivered me from all harm—may he bless these boys. May they be called by my name and the names of my fathers, Abraham and Isaac, and may they greatly increase upon the earth." (Gen. 48:16)

SAMSON AND DELILAH
Judges 13-16

We seem to be caught in a series of peaks and valleys in our great love stories. We ended the story of Adam and Eve somewhat in a valley east of Eden. We reached our first peak with Abraham and Sarah. Then Isaac and Rebekah plunged us deep into the valley of dysfunctional relationships. But we were rescued with the beautiful story of Jacob and Rachel, and to a lesser extent, Jacob and Leah. In our next chapter, we will scale the peaks again with the story of Ruth and Boaz, but first—in keeping with our pattern of peaks and valleys— we must plunge deep, deep into the abyss of "not-so-great" love stories with the infamous tale of Samson and Delilah. A little updating will help us to understand how we got to this point.

As we have already noted, Jacob (also known as Israel) had 12 sons. One of these sons, Joseph, is sold by his brothers into slavery in Egypt where, through the strength of his character and his favor with God, he becomes the second most powerful man in the country. He convinces his brothers and his father to also move to Egypt, where the family (now known as the children of Israel or Hebrews) stays for four hundred years. Eventually their status in society declines until they are mere slaves.

Then comes one of the true giants of history, Moses, who along with his successor Joshua, leads the children of Israel out of Egypt and into the Promised Land. However, the Philistines are still occupying the land; it takes many generations for the Promised Land to fall completely under Israel's control. During this chaotic time Israel is ruled by a series of Judges. You may recognize some of the names: Gideon, Deborah and Barak. Samson was the last of the judges whose name is known. He led, or judged, Israel for 20 years.

The time of the Judges was a time of great lawlessness. The author of Judges closes the book with these words: "In those days [there was] no king in Israel; everyone did [what was] right in his own eyes." (21:25)

Well, you can imagine what our land would be like if "everyone did [what was] right in his own eyes." Anarchy. We have enough moral confusion as it is. Our land might be considered somewhat tame in comparison to Canaan in the tumultuous times of the judges.

Our story begins on a high note. An angel of the Lord appears to a man named Manoah and his wife, telling them God is about to bless them with a son. Manoah is of the tribe of Dan, from the southern coastal lands adjacent to the Philistine territory, today known as Gaza. Here's something to think about: Only twice in the Old Testament did an angel foretell a person's birth. This honor was reserved for Isaac and for Samson, and both of them were disappointments as men. This is not to say that they were not used of God. They most certainly were, but it was almost as if God used them in spite of themselves.

Like some of the more famous couples before them, Samson's parents had tried for years to have children, but couldn't. Now their dream would come true. The angel had told them so. There were, however, some strings attached. The angel explained, "This son is to be reared to be totally dedicated to God. He is also to be reared under a Nazirite vow. He will do great deeds for your country in service to God."

To be reared under a Nazirite vow meant that he was forbidden from cutting his hair, eating raisins or grapes, drinking wine, and touching a dead body.

Notice that Samson didn't choose to be a Nazirite. Ordinarily, a person would take the Nazirite vow later on in life, generally for only a short term. But Samson was chosen to be a Nazirite from his birth. Maybe this explains some of the contradictions in his life. Step back from Scripture for a moment and think about the burden it puts upon a child to say to that child, "You are a special child. God has laid His hand on you. You are different from other children. Here are some of the ways that you are to live to show that you are different."

Some children might respond quite well to this. Read the story of Samuel when you have a chance and you will encounter such a child. Can you see, however, that some children might rebel? Can you also see that, even in the midst of that rebellion, such a child might still sense God's special calling in his or her life? Judges 13:25 says that "the Spirit of the Lord began to take hold of [Samson]."

This is one of the first times in the Bible where it is recorded that a person has the presence of the Spirit in their life. The Spirit of the Lord had come on Moses, Joshua, Deborah, Gideon, and now that same Spirit was stirring in Samson.

Having the Spirit come upon him did not keep Samson from making some dumb, dumb mistakes. However, it does give us a foreshadowing that, in spite of his many character weaknesses, God would use Samson to achieve God's ends.

In some ways Samson didn't have a chance as a kid. The expectations were so high. His parents named him "sun" or "brightness." That is what the name Samson means. His parents obviously had great dreams for him. And he was the strongest kid not only on his block, but on any block. No matter the sport, he was the star. Again, some kids handle that quite well, but can you see how it might breed arrogance?

Samson grows to manhood with the strength of several men. He wins great battles single-handedly against the Philistines. And yet, time after time, Samson is also very weak, giving in to his emotions or his passions instead of staying true to his Nazirite vows.

He falls in love with a Philistine woman from Timnah, even though such a relationship violates his faith. Try as they might, his devout parents can't talk him out of it. What do you do with a head-strong young person?

On the way to Timnah to make the wedding arrangements, a lion attacks Samson. Samson kills the beast with his bare hands, leaving its carcass behind.

As the wedding day approaches, Samson goes to Timnah again. This time as he walks past the carcass of the lion, he notices bees swarming around it. He reaches into the carcass, scooping out the honey it contained. He shares some of the honey with his parents, but neglects to tell them where it came from.

As a Nazirite, Samson was not supposed to ever touch a dead body, even that of an animal. By taking honey from the dead body of the lion, Samson broke his vows.

At the wedding feast, Samson poses a riddle to thirty of the guests and makes a wager with them that they cannot solve it. The wager went like this: "Out of the eater, something to eat; out of the strong, something sweet."

The men can't solve the riddle, so they approach Samson's bride and threaten to harm her and her father if she doesn't give them the answer. She begs Samson to tell her the answer, and Samson gives in. She passes it on to the wedding guests. In Judges 14:18 we read, "Before sunset on the seventh day the men of the town said to him, 'What is sweeter than honey? What is stronger than a lion?'"

Then Samson gave one of the most memorable, and I think humorous, retorts in all the Scriptures, "If you had not plowed with my heifer, you would not have solved my riddle." O. K., it's a little sexist, but you'll have to admit that Samson is one colorful figure. But he had lost his wager, and this made him a little ticked off.

The men of Timnah soon learn it isn't smart to make the strongest man on earth angry. In a fit of rage, Samson kills thirty other men in the village, strips them of their belongings, and gives their clothes to those who had explained the riddle. Then, says Judges 14:19, "Burning with anger, he went up to his father's house."

Doesn't that seem to be a mite bit of an overreaction? Just because somebody figures out your riddle, you kill thirty people? The man's a psycho. How could this man be a hero in any culture, especially the Bible?

A Jewish rabbi was explaining how Samson acquired his stature in the faith of Judaism. He suggested that Jewish boys and girls needed this kind of superhero to look up to, since Jews are usually known more for their brains than their brawn. It's like the old joke about the number of Jewish players in the NBA. (They're far exceeded by the number who are team owners.)

Samson is out of control, but he is not even close to touching bottom. He returns to Timnah to claim his wife, and discovers that his father-in-law has given her to his best man. Now Samson is really ticked off! He captures 300 foxes and ties their tails together in pairs with a torch between them. After lighting the torches, Samson releases them into the fields of the Philistines. Where is the ASPCA when you need it? Now the Philistines are ticked off. Who can blame them? They kill his bride and her father. This makes Samson even more furious, and he exacts revenge, killing more of the Philistines.

Then Samson's own people turn on him. They tie him with new ropes and take him to the Philistines. But Samson breaks free and kills one thousand of the Philistines with the jaw bone of a donkey. It sounds like an Arnold Schwarzenegger movie, but it's in THE BOOK!

Then, when we think it can't get much worse, Judges 16:1 begins with these words, "One day Samson went to Gaza, where he saw a prostitute. He went in to spend the night with her." What's a good Nazirite boy doing with a prostitute? By this time, the Nazirite vow is in shreds.

While Samson is enjoying the charms of the prostitute, word gets around the city that the vile champion of the Hebrews is in town. So the Philistines try a new strategy. They lock the city gates. Now they have him trapped. But Samson tears the gates off their hinges and carries them to Hebron, nearly forty miles away! It's estimated that these gates may have weighed over a thousand pounds. Superhero is right! In those days the gates of a city were considered the symbol of its strength. By removing the city gate, Samson is the cause of a great deal of civic humiliation in Gaza.

Samson was a piece of work—the strongest man who ever lived on the outside, but a conflicted man with a ferocious temper and a weakness for women to match. He had no respect for his position as a Nazirite. He used his God-given strength indiscriminately. Like Esau, who sold his birthright for a bowl of stew, Samson had no respect for the gifts God had given him. And he is about to hit rock bottom.

Judges 16:4 begins this phase of our story so innocently, "Samson loved a woman in the valley of Sorek whose name was Delilah." Why can't the boy learn? Delilah's a Philistine. Remember the vow, Samson, before it's too late.

Her name in Hebrew means "weak," but don't be fooled, she was a bombshell (at least as portrayed by Hedy Lamarr in Cecil B. DeMille's 1949 hit movie, "Samson and Delilah"). And "weak" is a relative term. The strongest man on earth was certainly no match for her. Bible teacher Herbert Wolf explains it this way: "Rather than break his relationship with Delilah, he allowed it to break him."

What Samson doesn't know is that the Philistine leaders, who hate him (for good reason), have paid Delilah an enormous sum—fifty-five hundred pieces of silver in all—to betray him. Do you know how much that is in today's money? I don't know if you have priced an ounce of silver lately, but this was a princely payment. Delilah sets out to find the secret of Samson's great strength.

So begins an historic game of cat-and-mouse, as two seasoned deceivers engage in a battle of wits. First, Samson tells Delilah that if he were tied with seven fresh thongs that have not been dried, he would lose his strength. He lied.

The second time, Samson claims that if he were tied with a new rope that has never been used, he would lose his strength. He lied again.

Then, in the most bizarre lie of all, he tells her that if she would weave the seven braids of his hair into a fabric on the loom, and tighten it with the pin, he would become as weak as any other man. The fabric was just another fabrication.

Delilah is beside herself with frustration. "How can you say you love me when you won't confide in me?"

Samson finally weakens. He tells her everything. "No razor has ever been used on my head," he said, "because I have been a Nazirite set apart to God since birth. If my head were shaved, my strength would leave me, and I would become as weak as any other man."

Ironically, when the strong man finally tells the truth, it is his undoing. When Samson's head is shaved, he loses his strength. It was not Samson's hair that gave him strength, but his special relationship with God that was sealed before he was born. Now he had finally broken every thread of the Nazirite vow. He drank wine, he ate grapes, he touched a dead body. He did not dedicate himself to God. And now his hair, the outward sign of his spiritual grace, was gone. Verse 20 of the sixteenth chapter of Judges is regarded as among the saddest verses in Scripture: "But he did not know that the Lord had departed from him."

The Philistines easily overpower him and the result is brutal. Rather than merely imprisoning him, they gouge out his eyes and chain him to a huge stone wheel like an animal where he is forced to grind grain into flour. And they display him to the Philistine people who ridicule him and heap scorn on him. Their mighty adversary had fallen, and they would make the most of it.

It is a shame that the Philistines did not have the book of Judges to guide them. They would have been able to read verse 26 of the sixteenth chapter, one of the most ominous verses in all the Bible: "But the hair on [Samson's] head began to grow again."

The main god of the Philistines was called Dagon, their god of grain. They built a huge temple for Dagon where they went to make sacrifices to him and to have feasts. Now that this despised strong man was under their control, the Philistines decided to use him for public relations purposes. Three thousand of their political, military and religious elite were gathered for one such feast.

"While they were in high spirits, they shouted, 'Bring out Samson to entertain us.'"

Archeologists have uncovered Philistine temples built around the period of the Judges. Their construction design shows them having two large wooden columns on stone bases in the center of the building, supporting the roof. Samson says to the servant who is guiding him by the hand, "Put me where I can feel the pillars that support the temple, so that I may lean against them." So they drag Samson out of the prison, and force this blind, shackled, utterly disgraced man to perform for them.

Now Samson has hit rock bottom. And at this point, Samson turns to God. How sad that he waited until his life was a total wreck before he finally turned to the source of all his strength for help. Of course, Samson is not the first or the last to make that mistake. Out of a humbled heart, he breathes one final, desperate prayer:

"O Sovereign Lord, remember me. O God, please strengthen me just once more . . ."

And Samson begins to push against the massive pillars of the temple of Dagon. And as he pushes, this enormous temple begins to buckle and the roof caves in, and all three thousand of the greatest leaders of the Philistines are killed. As a consequence, the Philistine people were weakened, leading the way for their eventual defeat by the Israelites. Samson dies in the devastation as well, but he dies a hero's death. His family buries him with honor.

Samson was a golden boy whose life became progressively

tarnished. He was meant for great things. An angel announced his coming birth. His parents were devout people who sought God's wisdom in raising their son. From birth, he was set apart for holy service to God. Yet somehow, Samson never lived up to his potential. (How many parents lie awake at night and agonize over the question, "Where did we go wrong with our child?") Samson's failures were clearly not his parents' fault. He was a free moral agent, and he blew it.

Mark Twain once observed that "man is the only animal who blushes . . . and who needs to." Samson's life was an embarrassment to God, and yet God never gave up on him. And when Samson finally turned to God, God was there. That's my hope . . . and yours.

In his book, *People of the Lie*, Dr. M. Scott Peck writes about one of his most difficult counseling situations. It involved a woman he calls Charlene. At a crucial point in her counseling, right after she explained that everything in life seemed meaningless, Dr. Peck asked her what the purpose of life was to Christians.

"We exist for the glory of God," Charlene said in a flat, low monotone, as if she were sullenly repeating an alien catechism, learned by rote and extracted from her at gunpoint. "The purpose of our life is to glorify God."

"Well," Dr. Peck responded. There was a short silence. For a brief moment Peck thought she might cry.

"I cannot do it," she said. "There's no room for me in that. That would be my death." Then with a suddenness that frightened Peck, what seemed to be her choked-back sobs turned into a roar. "I don't want to live for God," she cried out. "I will not. I want to live for me. For my own sake!" [20]

Samson was not the first person or the last to reject God's call. He broke the vows that were made in his behalf before his birth. He chose a life of pleasure and violence. He made his own rules, went his own way. And God did not interfere in his life in any way. And Samson paid dearly for his transgressions.

Still, God is a God of grace and forgiveness. There is Samson's name in the New Testament in the eleventh chapter of Hebrews in the Bible's Gallery of Heroes. And he is listed as a man of faith.

God is a gracious God. God can forgive any sin, redeem any sinner, but how much better it is when God finds people of character who are willing to live to the glory of God. It's time to leave Samson, this tragic hero, who broke himself on God's laws, but turned to God in the end and was used by God to help deliver the Promised Land to the people of Israel. Now it is time for another peak experience, perhaps the highest peak romantically speaking in the Hebrew Bible. Refresh your mind with the beautiful story of Ruth and Boaz. That's next.

RUTH AND BOAZ
Ruth 1-4

Our next love story is one of the few truly wholesome love stories of the Bible. Famed radio Bible teacher J. Vernon McGee says, "The Book of Ruth is a pearl in the swine pen of the Judges."

As you remember from our last chapter, the time of the Judges, was a time of moral chaos when, "[there was] no king in Israel; everyone did [what was] right in his own eyes." (Judges 21:25) And yet, in the middle of a corrupt and hedonistic culture, we find this little pearl of a story about a family of love and character.

Let's set the stage for our story with a little detour to the world of contemporary country music.

As you know, some of the most popular music today comes out of places like Nashville, Tennessee and Austin, Texas. I am referring, of course, to Country and Western music. Country music is known for its colorful lyrics.

We're told that former Supreme Court Justice William O. Douglas was a country music fan. He delighted in recounting the titles of his favorite songs. Among them were, "When the Phone Don't Ring, You'll Know It's Me," "Walk Out Backwards, So I'll Think You're Coming In," and "My Wife Ran Off with My Best Friend, and I Sure Do Miss Him." These gems were found in an album titled "Songs I Learned at My Mother's Knee, and at Other Joints." [21]

One sentimental country song popular a few years ago was

titled, "A Long Line of Love." It tells of a young man who is getting married. His sweetheart asks him if he thinks they can make it. His answer is "I come from a long line of love."

Then he talks about his parents' marriage and his grandparents' marriage, and at the end of each refrain he sings, "Forever's in my heart and in my blood . . . I come from a long line of love." [22]

As we go through this love story, I believe you will come to see that Jesus of Nazareth also came from a long line of love, as do you and I.

Our story begins with a family of four—a man named Elimelech; his wife, Naomi; and their two sons, Mahlon and Kilion. They lived in Bethlehem. Like many families today, this family was experiencing economic difficulties. A famine had spread throughout their land, and food was scarce. So Elimelech and Naomi packed up a small U-Haul and moved from Bethlehem to a place called Moab, where there was more food.

They spent approximately ten years in Moab. During this time both sons met Moabite women and married them. Such marriages were not kosher (literally), as you might expect. But there is no sign that Elimelech and Naomi showed any antagonism toward their sons' choices. Things were difficult, but they were surviving. Then all of a sudden, Elimelech died as did their two sons. Like many women who are widowed much too young, Naomi was devastated.

Opportunities for women in that day and time were practically non-existent. Naomi was left all alone in a foreign country. All she had left were two daughters-in-law. How would she possibly get by?

The only viable option was for her to return to her hometown and hope there would be a place for her somewhere among her relatives. And thus she and her two daughters-in-law set out for the land of Judah.

As the three widows began their journey, it occurred to Naomi that it might be better for her daughters-in-law to remain in their own country. She loved her daughters-in-law, and she wanted to see them happy. So she encouraged them to go back to their mothers' house. They were still young; they could find new husbands and have the security she could not give them.

However, Ruth and Orpah, her daughters-in-law, wanted to stay with Naomi. Naomi knew the challenges they would face; these women would not be accepted by her relatives in her home country. The law was very clear about such things. The Hebrews viewed Moabites as bitter enemies. The Moabites were the descendants of Lot from his incestuous relationship with his oldest daughter. Thus they were particularly disgusting to the Jews. According to Deuteronomy 23:3, no Moabite shall "enter into the congregation of the Lord; even to their tenth generation."

If her daughters-in-law remained with her, they would never be accepted among her people. So Naomi encouraged them to stay in their homeland. She told them that it was absurd for them to follow her, "Do I still have sons in my womb that they may become your husbands?" she asked them.

Finally, Orpah decided that her mother-in-law was right. It would be best for her to remain in her own country. Daughter-in-law Ruth, however, still wanted to remain with Naomi. Ruth loved Naomi deeply. It was in this context that Ruth spoke some of the most famous words in all of literature: "Entreat me not to leave thee, Or to return from following after thee: For whither thou goest, I will go; And where thou lodgest, I will lodge; Thy people shall be my people, And thy God my God: Where thou diest, I will die, And there will I be buried: The Lord do so to me, and more also, If ought but death part thee and me. (Ruth 1: 16-17, KJV)

The story of Ruth and Naomi is what love is about. It is about loyalty and faithfulness and mutual devotion.

A three-year-old girl became critically ill. She spent months in the hospital, where her mother kept a constant vigil by her bedside. A petite woman, weighing little more than ninety pounds, this mother stayed right with her daughter day and night, displaying an amazing strength which inspired her family and friends.

Eventually the little girl recovered. Once she was home, everyone asked her mother how she had done it. How could anyone have the strength to do what she did? The young mother smiled warmly, and told her questioners, "She's my child. I love her more than breathing. She needed me. She needed me as never before. I had to do it. I had to be there for her!" [23]

That's love, isn't it? It's not, "I love you for what you can do for me." Or "I'll love you as long as it is convenient."

No.

It's, "I'll love you no matter what. I'll always be there."

In the classic Russian novel *Crime and Punishment*, a young student murders two people for their money. He rationalizes his crime by telling himself, first, that Napoleon killed thousands and became a hero; second, that his victims were unimportant people; and third, that he would use the money to further his career for the good of humanity. Most of the story, however, is taken up not with the crime but with the young student's punishment—punishment not from without, but from within. Guilt rages inside, and his body, mind, and spirit grind away at each other and wear him down.

There is a young girl in the novel, Sonia, who loves this murderer. Hers is a rare kind of love. It is not cheap sentiment. First of all, her love drives him to confess that he is the murderer. She tells him he must do penance to try and expiate his guilt. He does. He kisses the ground he has stained with human blood and cries out his confession to the four corners of the earth. Finally he is convicted and sent off to Siberia, suffering from tuberculosis and pneumonia. But the story doesn't end there. The girl, Sonia, follows him over the hard miles to Siberia.

Throughout his nine-year sentence, she stays by his side. She keeps them both alive by scrounging whatever food she can find. Her love never quits. *Crime and Punishment* is about real love. [24]

Could Hollywood produce such a film today? I'm not sure it could. The values of our society have changed too much. First of all, here is a man feeling the weight of his guilt who confesses his crime for the sake of his soul. What does Hollywood know about such despair? And here is someone who loves him so much that she causes him to face up to his wrongdoing and then sticks by him through all the subsequent punishment. Hollywood would never buy it. It's out of touch with where we are. It's about faith and values and undying loyalty. That is what *real* love is.

I wonder, as young couples stand before the altar and light the Ruth candle in their wedding ceremonies, if they understand the love of Ruth for Naomi? Ruth was committed to her mother-in-law even when there was nothing for her to gain and everything to lose.

So these two women set out for Bethlehem, Naomi's hometown. Naomi's relatives greeted her fondly as they entered the city. But she told them, "Don't call me Naomi. Call me Mara," which means *bitter*, "for my life has been a bitter one."

Life is not much better for Ruth and Naomi in Bethlehem than it had been in Moab. The only food Naomi and Ruth had to eat was what was left in the farmers' fields after harvest. This system was known as "gleaning." In the book of Leviticus, God instructed the farmers of Israel not to take all of the grain out of the field or all the grapes off of the vines, but to leave some there for the poor. Farmers were not permitted to go over their fields a second time. Also, workers were instructed not to harvest the corners of their fields. Whatever was left from the first harvest was to remain for the widows and poor to collect. Without that charitable law many of the poor would doubtless have starved.

In Deuteronomy 15, God instructs the people of Israel to deal generously with the poor. There is that recognition that while some people are poor because they refuse to work, most are the victims of circumstances over which they have no control. Still, gleaning the fields was humiliating and arduous work to which only the very poor and needy would stoop.

Ruth goes to work gleaning in the field of a wealthy man named Boaz. It is not long until Ruth catches Boaz' eye. She is different from the other women, more graceful and lovely to look at. Boaz inquires after her. When he learns of Ruth's devotion to Naomi, her mother-in-law, he is even more impressed. He instructs his men not to harm Ruth and to make sure enough grain is left over so that she might gather it with ease.

Boaz even invites Ruth to have lunch with him. "Come over here," he says: "Have some bread and dip it in the wine vinegar" (v. 14). A little later, he offers her some roasted grain. Not exactly a meal at the Ritz, but still it was a gesture he did not offer to the other women gleaning in his field.

Naomi has not been a disinterested spectator in all of this. In fact, there is evidence that Naomi has been subtly guiding Ruth toward this relationship all along. She informs Ruth that Boaz' name means "standing in strength," and that he is a close relative. Then she introduces a most interesting concept. She calls Boaz their "kinsman-redeemer."

Deuteronomy 25:5-10 spells out the responsibilities of a kinsman-redeemer. If a married man dies, the closest male relative is called upon to protect the interests of the family. If the dead man has no children, the kinsman-redeemer is to marry the widow and bear children with her to carry on the man's name. He is also called upon to buy back the land of the poorer relative if it has been sold to satisfy a debt, so that the family inheritance is protected.

And so Naomi continues her efforts as match-maker. She makes it clear that if this relationship with Boaz moves forward, Ruth must take the lead. It was at the end of the harvest season. Boaz would be taking his wheat to the threshing floor. The threshing floor was located outside the city. Boaz would be spending the night there.

Naomi tells Ruth to wash herself, dress in her best clothes, put on some perfume, and go to Boaz' tent. While Boaz slept, she was to "uncover his feet." Some scholars suggest this is an euphemism for a more earthy approach. Whatever the nature of this gesture, it was within the cultural mores of Ruth's time. When Boaz woke, if he spread his skirt or cloak over Ruth, this would signify that he was accepting her offer.

My guess is that Naomi knew how Boaz would respond. He responded like a gentleman. Boaz was substantially older than Ruth; he is grateful that she chose him when she could have found a younger man. He indicates that he is ready to fulfill the kinsman-redeemer role, but he knows that there is another relative who is even more closely related to the family who has first claim on that role. He promises Ruth that if the other man declines, then he will gladly fulfill his role.

But Boaz is also concerned about more immediate matters. He is concerned about Ruth's reputation. He tells her to wait until morning to leave so she will not be spied traipsing around at night.

The next morning he instructs his workers to tell no one about her visit. He gives Ruth six measures of barley so that, if anyone does see her, she will have a legitimate excuse for being at the threshing floor. This is important since, during Biblical times, threshing floors were associated with sexual activity, particularly that of prostitutes (Hosea 9). Notice through all of this that Boaz shows himself to be a man of character. He does not take advantage of the situation, but instead, at each step, he does the honorable thing.

He tells Ruth that he will talk to the closer relative and will settle the matter, which he does. A few days later Boaz meets the relative at the city gate. This was a common setting for settling business transactions. There was heavy foot traffic, as people would travel in and out of the town at the gate. Boaz calls together ten elders of the city to serve as witnesses. He explains the situation and gives the relative the opportunity to do his duty as kinsman-redeemer. However, the relative is not excited by the offer. If he married Ruth and had a son by her, then all of their property might revert to Elimelech's family. And this was not what he wanted, so he refused.

Having done his part to satisfy the demands of his culture, Boaz takes Ruth to be his wife. What a great story, but we're only getting started.

Ruth bears a son in her new hometown of Bethlehem, and she names this precious son Obed. Obed, in turn, fathers a son named Jesse. And one of Jesse's sons became Israel's most famous king, David. And David was an ancestor of another baby boy born in Bethlehem many years later named . . . Jesus of Nazareth.

Isn't it interesting that in the lineage of Jesus there is a woman who was a despised Moabite? She is there because of her character and the character of her husband and her loyalty to her mother-in-law. Do you see now why I say that Jesus came from a long line of love?

And so do we. That kind of love is what the cross is about. It is about a love that never quits, never gives up, never fails. It is *agape* love—love from the heart of God. It's not, "I love you for what you can do for me;" or "I'll love you as long as it is convenient." It's, "I'll love you no matter what. I'll always be there for you." And you and I are the recipients of that love. There is a red ribbon that extends from our lives all the way back to Calvary. Over the past two thousand years people just like us have believed in that love, and they've passed that love on. Through plagues and famines, oftentimes under barbaric oppression, they did not let go of it. And we are the recipients of that love.

We come from a long line of love. It would be tragic if in our modern obsession with the satisfactions of the moment, we should allow that ribbon to become frayed and finally to break.

Virginia Duran was born in a migrant worker camp in central California. Her father was in jail, and her mother could not afford to raise a child. She was named after a kindly woman doctor who helped the family by finding them food and clothing, and by paying their rent. A few years after Virginia's birth, the family moved, and the young girl lost contact with that caring doctor.

Years later, when Virginia was grown, she was visiting Mexico when she saw a picture of a poor girl in the newspaper. At that moment, Virginia realized that she might have shared that little girl's fate if it hadn't been for the intervention of her benefactor, the doctor.

Virginia and her sister decided that they would pass on this legacy of caring to other needy children. The two sisters traveled to Mexico and found a dusty village filled with migrant children, many of them malnourished or sick. Many of the children's parents were unwed teenagers or alcoholics. Virginia and her sister did what they could to provide for the children's basic needs. Today, they have 35 children in their care.

As Virginia was taking care of the children one day, she suddenly remembered something she had long forgotten. Doctor Virginia once told her that she, the doctor, had been rescued by a wealthy woman herself. Her benefactor had also been saved from poverty by yet another woman, who had been rescued by another woman—back six generations. All of these women lived in the west, and all were surrogate mothers for children who desperately needed love. Interestingly, all of the women were named Virginia.

"You're the seventh in a long line," the doctor told her. "And someday, you'll do as much for someone else." [25]

Virginia Duran came from a long line of love.

So did Jesus. So do you and I. It is the Love that says, "I love you—not because I need you but because you are you. I will always be there no matter what." That is God's love.

"Forever's in our heart and in our blood; we come from a long line of love."

But there is another fascinating twist to this story. It concerns Ruth's husband, Boaz. We've already noted that he was a wealthy landowner, and that he was a man of sterling character. Did you know, however, that his mother was a prostitute? You've heard her name before. His mother was Rahab, the harlot. Under Mosaic Law Rahab the prostitute could have been stoned to death for her sins, but instead she occupies an honored place in Israel's history.

You may remember her story which you'll find in the book of Joshua. Joshua sent spies into the Promised Land. They came to Rahab the harlot and she hid them. She said to the spies, "I know that the

Lord has given this land to you" (Josh 2:9)—one of the Bible's great statements of faith.

Rahab risked her life to protect the Israelite spies, and she asked only one thing in return—that her family be spared when the Israelite army occupied the land. Rahab's family was spared, and she was handsomely rewarded. Her son became a wealthy landowner. Even more importantly, he became the husband of Ruth and the great grandfather of Israel's most powerful and renowned king. And, more importantly than all of this, Boaz was an ancestor of the King of Kings. Imagine, one of Jesus ancestors was a prostitute and another a despised Moabite. This is a story of grace, God's grace. These people became heroes of the Bible, not by their own merit, but by their faith in the providence of God. It is also a story of diversity in the middle of an Old Testament culture of exclusivity. And it is a story of love—pure love, faithful love, unselfish love.

It is said that when Benjamin Franklin was ambassador to France, he often met with a group of intellectuals who disparaged the Bible. On one occasion Franklin said, "By the way, gentlemen, I have come across a most intriguing love story that I would like to read for you tonight. I think you'll find it interesting." He then proceeded to read to them a hand-written copy of the book of Ruth.

After he finished the four short chapters, his audience was ecstatic. "That is the greatest love story we have ever heard," they exclaimed. "You must publish it at once."

Franklin answered, "It has been published. It is in the Bible."

It is one of the greatest love stories ever penned: "A pearl in the swine pit of the Judges."

DAVID AND BATHSHEBA
II Samuel 11: 1 to I Chronicles 3:5

Generally, Jewish people did not include women in their genealogies. They considered the male, not the female, as the one who kept the family line alive. Only five women are mentioned in the genealogy of Jesus and only in Matthew's Gospel. We've already mentioned two of them. Here's the entire list: Tamar, who tricked Judah; Rahab the harlot; Ruth, the Moabite woman who married Boaz; Bathsheba, the lover and later the wife of David; and Mary, Jesus' mother.

Here is what is interesting about Bathsheba—she is the only one not mentioned by name. It is as if she is the only one who was never forgiven by the people of Israel. We can understand that. The relationship between David and Bathsheba was the greatest stain on David's record and David was Israel's favorite king.

Bathsheba was the wife of Uriah, one of King David's most loyal soldiers. "One evening David got up from his bed and walked around on the roof. . ." Was David having trouble sleeping? Was he, like many men who reach middle age, occasionally plagued by sleepless nights full of worries about who he really was and what his life was really worth? Did this put him in a more susceptible frame of mind when he spotted Bathsheba?

The Scripture writer hints that David was in Jerusalem with too much time on his hands when he should have been out in the field with his troops. Boredom has wreaked havoc in many people's lives.

Whatever the case, David saw Bathsheba out on her rooftop bathing and he saw that she was very beautiful. Though he knew she was married, he sent messengers to invite her to the palace. She came to him, and he slept with her.

What was Bathsheba doing out there bathing on her roof? She may have been engaged in a Jewish ritual bath, a mikvah, when David spotted her. The Bible makes it clear that she had just cleansed herself after her time of uncleanness (menstruation). The reason the writer mentioned this may be to prove that she was not already pregnant before she slept with David.

We get no indication that Bathsheba was an unwilling partner in this relationship, though there was a definite imbalance of power, and David probably was exploiting his role as king.

After their affair, Bathsheba returns home. Sometime later she sends a chilling message to the King: "I'm pregnant."

According to the Law, both David and Bathsheba could have received the death penalty for their sin. (Lev. 20:10, Deut. 22:22) But David was the king. It is not unusual in any society for there to be two sets of rules—one for the common people and one for the power elite.

Remember Bathsheba was married to Uriah, one of David's most loyal soldiers. This makes their relationship even more odious. David summons Uriah to his palace. He makes small talk, then suggests that Uriah go home and relax after his hard work on the battlefield. He even sends along a gift of royal food, hoping this might put Uriah in a relaxed mood. Obviously, he wants Uriah to go home and make love to his wife Bathsheba. But Uriah feels a loyalty to his troops and remains with the other soldiers and servants rather than going home. We can attribute this to his sterling character, or we might attribute this to some reluctance on Uriah's part to spend time with his wife. Maybe if he had been more attentive to Bathsheba . . . .

At any rate, Uriah's faithfulness to his men stands in sharp contrast to David's behavior. It is clear that adultery is a serious transgression, even for a king. David is getting desperate to cover it up. He gets Uriah drunk, in the hopes that this will make Uriah forget his duties and return to his wife. But Uriah still insists on sleeping out in the fields with the soldiers.

Finally, David draws up Uriah's death sentence. He writes an order to his commander, Joab, to put Uriah on the front lines of battle, and then to withdraw so that Uriah will be killed. Joab does as he is told. David has disposed of his problem but at a terrible cost.

In 1990, in San Jose, California, over 400 firefighters spent hours battling a major fire that was set by a man trying to burn his garbage. Garbage-burning is illegal in most states. The offender, Luke Goodrich, had only intended to start a small fire in order to incinerate one pile of garbage. He had no idea the fire would rage out of control and cause so much destruction.

But he should have foreseen the possible consequences of his actions—because Luke Goodrich is one of the captains of the San Jose fire department!

Like a fireman unwisely burning garbage, once a person deliberately chooses to sin, he or she often loses control of the consequences of sin. Like King David, we may discover too late that our sins can take us on a path that is far outside of God's will.

After the acceptable period of mourning has passed, David marries Bathsheba, but, says the writer of II Samuel, "the Lord was displeased with them." David got what he wanted, but never again would his life be marked by God's blessings and peace.

The prophet Nathan confronts David about his sin. This bold prophet uses a parable about two men, a wealthy cattle owner and a poor man. The poor man had only a small lamb to care for, and it meant all the world to him. But the wealthy cattle owner selfishly took the poor man's lamb and killed it for a meal.

King David is incensed by this story. It isn't fair! It isn't right for the wealthy man to take the poor man's only lamb, and he demands justice for the poor man. At this point, Nathan reveals that the parable is about King David himself. God had given David abundant blessings. Yet David had taken Uriah's wife. Even though Uriah died in battle, Nathan makes it clear that David is guilty of murder.

And Nathan issues a prophecy from God (II Sam. 12:10): "Now, therefore, the sword will never depart from your house, because you despised me and took the wife of Uriah the Hittite to be your own." Nathan also prophesies that David's wives will be taken away and given to another.

David recognizes his sin right away and confesses it. Even though he deserves death according to the Law, Nathan informs him that God will not kill him. Instead, the child which Bathsheba carries in her body will die.

Can you imagine bearing that knowledge? Can you imagine knowing that you were responsible for the death of your own child? Like any of us, David probably would have preferred to die himself rather than face the knowledge that his sin had resulted in his child's death.

For seven days, David fasts and prays for this child. The elders of the household urge him to eat, but he refuses. On the seventh day, the child dies. At first, the servants are afraid to tell David. But when he hears the news, David does something significant: He gets up, cleans himself up, and goes to worship. He is showing his acceptance of his understanding of God's will.

People who have experienced it say that the death of a child is the worst pain a person can endure. How do you think the death of this child affected David and Bathsheba as a couple? Have you ever tried worshiping God when you are in great pain?

Later, David and Bathsheba have another son whom they name Solomon. Solomon's name means "peace." Nathan the prophet informs them that God wants them to also name the child Jedidiah, which means "loved by the Lord." God, in His infinite graciousness, is revealing His blessing on this child's life. And David has several other offspring by his other wives.

Unfortunately, Nathan's prophecy concerning David's sin has not run its course: Amnon, one of David's sons, lusts after his half-sister Tamar. He and his friend, Jonadab, draw up a plan to trap her. Amnon pretends to be ill and asks David to send Tamar to his room to feed him. When Tamar arrives, Amnon rapes her. The rape is horrible in itself, but this is also incest, and the loss of Tamar's virginity means that she can never be married.

Tamar goes into mourning, and moves into the home of her brother, Absalom. Absalom is furious and plots revenge against Amnon.

In the meantime, David does nothing to punish Amnon. Had the memory of his own sins caused him to lose moral authority in his household?

A few years ago, *Time* magazine did an article on how today's parents have problems talking to their children about drugs, because so many of the parents had used drugs when they were teens. These parents now felt that they have no moral authority to tell their kids to "just say no" when they had indulged in their youth. Was this the dilemma David found himself in?

Two years later, Absalom sets his wicked plan in motion. The time of sheep-shearing was an occasion to celebrate. Absalom invites all his brothers and half-brothers and his father, David, to a party. David declines the invitation, but sends Amnon in his place (at Absalom's urging). The wine flows freely, and Amnon gets drunk. At Absalom's signal, his men attack Amnon and kill him. Now Absalom has his revenge; the murder also clears the way for Absalom to take over David's throne. Nevertheless Absalom flees fearing David's wrath. Amnon is dead and Absalom has fled, so David has lost his two oldest sons.

For three years, Absalom stays away, and David longs for him. Once more, David does not punish his son for his sin. I Kings 1:6 makes it clear that David was a not a hands-on kind of parent. He did not discipline his children or involve himself in their lives. This may explain why they were so arrogant and disrespectful to him.

In II Samuel 16:22, Absalom—who is trying to destroy David and replace him on the throne—rapes David's concubines while David is away. He does this to insult and shame his father. Absalom rebels completely against David and tries to seize his throne. But God is still watching over David's kingdom. Absalom dies an untimely and gruesome death. For the third time in his life, King David mourns the death of a child.

II Samuel 22 and 23 give us a glimpse into David's character in his old age. He is once again seeking to live a righteous life. He acknowledges all the Lord has done for him. He takes responsibility for his sins and asks God to strike him, rather than his people (II Samuel 24: 10-17).

King David is growing old and feeble. His young son, Adonijah, tries to usurp the throne, bypassing David's right to name a successor. (I Kings 1: 5-6)

The prophet Nathan advises Bathsheba to go in to David and inform him of Adonijah's plan in order to save herself and her son Solomon, who was meant to succeed David.

Not long before his death, David re-affirms his oath to

Bathsheba that her son, Solomon, would take the throne. Then, he arranges for a public proclamation to that effect. It is evident that over the years Bathsheba has earned a place of influence and respect with him. If only they had met under different circumstances. If only they had not violated God's law. But they did, and the consequences were heart-breaking.

But notice that even though David was unfaithful to God, God never gave up on David. God never withdrew His promises to David. And one day, God would pay David the greatest compliment of all—Jesus of Nazareth, King of Kings and Lord of Lords, was born of the house and lineage of David. This was why Mary and Joseph were guided to Bethlehem by the Roman taxation, for Bethlehem was David's hometown. It is a huge reminder that God is a God of grace. That was David's salvation—and that is yours and mine as well.

An imagined conversation between David and Bathsheba after the death of their first child:

Bathsheba *(angry)*: "I see you're finally eating . . . So, how does it feel?"

David *(numb)*: "How does what feel?"

Bathsheba: "How does it feel to know that your God rejected your prayers? This has never happened to you before, has it? The great King David, he can do no wrong! God is on his side. Your God has always blessed you, always protected you, always delivered the enemy into your hands. But not this time. Why was this prayer any different? The God who could save a small boy from a giant couldn't save the life of one innocent baby. Someone explain that to me!"

David: "Don't blame God. Blame me. My child paid for my sin. Don't blame God."

Bathsheba: "So once more, the great King David is protected by his God. He doesn't even have to pay for his own sins."

David: "*Our* sins, Bathsheba. And that's not fair."

Bathsheba: "Not fair? Don't talk to me about fairness. My child is dead!"

David: "He was my child, too. . . . Do you know what I was praying for these last seven days? I begged God to take me instead. But God's justice is beyond our understanding. Blessed be the name of the Lord."

(Bathsheba, seeing David's grief, softens towards him. She walks over and wraps her arms around him.)

Bathsheba: "Blessed be the name of the Lord."

David: "I just hope the Lord hasn't removed His hand entirely from my life. I hope He can still use me . . . for something." — Angela Akers

ESTHER AND XERXES
Esther 1 - 10

Kick off your shoes for this story—it's one of the most delightful stories in all of literature. We've sampled romances from the time of the patriarchs, the Judges, and the Kings. Now it's time for a different kind of love story.

Our Jewish friends refer to it as the *Megillah*. It's a story that is read by the Jewish people on the eve and morning of the festival of Purim, which is celebrated in late winter. Purim commemorates an occasion when God delivered the Jewish people from the hands of those who sought to annihilate them.

Interestingly the book of Esther does not mention the name of God. You may recall that during the 2012 presidential campaign there was an uproar when the Democratic National Convention party platform contained no references to God. Perhaps representatives of the Democratic Party should have offered as their defense that the Bible has a book in it that does not mention God. Neither does the book of Esther mention such staples of Jewish history as Jerusalem, the law, the prophets, the Promised Land, the exile, as well as not mentioning God. Still, God's hand is very much evident throughout this delightful story.

I've always felt that somebody ought to turn the book of Esther into a Broadway musical. The book has everything. Besides romance, it has comedy. It has suspense. And it even has a villain, a man named Haman. Picture him with a long sinister-looking mustache which he twirls whenever he is pondering mischief. Haman's grievous flaw was that of vanity. He was a man who constantly needed his ego fed. And this extreme vanity caused him to involve himself in a most fiendish plot.

Comedian Louise O'Brien once claimed she knew a guy who was so conceited that he called Dial-A-Prayer and asked for his messages. That description would match Haman perfectly.

We're told that in synagogues and temples, during the celebration of Purim whenever the name of this villain Haman is uttered, the children make a racket of boos and jeers while they spin ratchety noisemakers. In some communities, Haman's name is written upon the soles of shoes, so that his name may literally be wiped out! [31] If you like your villains to be over-the-top and yet totally ineffectual, Haman is your man.

There is one thing more the story of Esther has. In keeping with today's world, it has loads of violence (which we are going to omit). Interestingly enough, it is not Haman that is the instigator of this violence (though he tries). Rather, it is our heroes, Esther and Mordecai.

The story takes place in Susa, the capital city of Persia quite late in the fifth century B. C., about 40 years before Nehemiah returned to Jerusalem to rebuild the walls of that holy city. Approximately 100 years earlier, Nebuchadnezzar, the king of Babylon, captured Jerusalem. He took many of the Jews back to Babylon during a period we know as the Babylonian exile. About 70 years later, the king of Persia defeated Babylon in battle. Soon afterwards, the Persians allowed the Jews to return to their own land, but not many went back. They had grown accustomed to their new land. When the story of Esther opens, most of the Jews are still living in Persia where some of them are doing quite well.

Our story begins with the King of the Persian Empire, a man named Xerxes (also called Ahasuerus in some versions of the Bible). Historians tell us that Xerxes was the son of King Darius. For you Bible scholars, Darius was the King who had Daniel thrown into the lions' den.

In our story Xerxes comes off as somewhat of a buffoon, but the Scripture tells us he was a powerful king who ruled over a vast land stretching from India to Ethiopia. In the third year of his reign, Xerxes decided to host a huge banquet for all the princes and governors of his empire. This was not a celebration lasting one or two days, but one showcasing his extreme wealth lasting six months. The last week of the celebration was open to everyone in the city and it was spectacular. Wine flowed freely, which happens quite frequently in the book of Esther. This partially explains some of the dumb things people do in this story.

While Xerxes entertained the men, his wife Queen Vashti hosted a separate extravaganza for women. Evidently Vashti was a strong woman with a mind of her own. On the last day of the banquet, when Xerxes was exhibiting a severe case of stupor from excessive drinking, he summoned Queen Vashti to join his party. His purpose was to show off her beauty. Some scholars say that he wanted her to dance naked before his guests, which might have given the Queen pause about accepting his invitation.

Anyway, at this point Vashti did something quite remarkable. She said, "No way." She declined the King's invitation.

At this, Xerxes became irate. Obviously he was not accustomed to people telling him, "No." After the banquet was concluded he consulted with his advisors about Vashti's intolerable disobedience.

His advisors agreed quite readily that the Queen's behavior could not be tolerated. One advisor cautioned the King that if he allowed this behavior to go unpunished, wives throughout the empire would start treating their husbands with contempt. It was suggested that, to forestall this kind of domestic revolution, the Queen be banished from the empire. This, in this advisor's opinion would guarantee respect for husbands in every household.

King Xerxes and the other advisors agreed. And thus a decree was sent out to all the empire that men should be supreme rulers over their own households (good luck with that!) So the decree went out and a kingdom-wide rebellion was averted.

Later, however, the King began having second thoughts. He suddenly realized his rash actions left him without a companion and a queen. The nights were getting cold and he was feeling a mite lonely. He could not, of course, reverse his decision and ask Vashti to come back, but it did make him sad.

Seeing the King's distress, an aid suggested they begin a search among the empire's beautiful young virgins for a substitute for Queen Vashti. Xerxes was of course delighted with this suggestion. He grew eager to implement this search for a new companion. He particularly delighted in imagining all the beautiful young women who would be brought to him for his approval. Immediately he sent his advisors out to find the most beautiful girl in all the land.

As you have already undoubtedly guessed, one of the girls selected to participate in this Miss Persia contest was a young Jewish girl by the name of Esther, also known among her people as Hadassah.

Scholars suggest that the name Esther may be derived from the Persian word for star. Esther was a star. Though she was young, she proved herself to be not only beautiful, but also resourceful. The contest, of course, did not take such things as resourcefulness into account. Nor did it require proficiency in such things as physics, literature or music. I. Q. was not a matter of concern. Only appearance seems to have mattered in this time of extreme male insensitivity.

Esther had a guardian, a wise and devout man by the name of Mordecai. Mordecai and Esther were cousins. After her parents died, Mordecai, who was quite a bit older than Esther, adopted and cared for his young cousin.

The Scriptures describe Esther in less than ten words. "She had a lovely figure and was beautiful." In other words she was eminently qualified to be the new Queen.

With her outstanding beauty it was no surprise that Esther was selected to participate as one of the candidates in the process of selecting a successor to Queen Vashti. This would require Esther to be away from Mordecai's oversight for at least a year. However, before she left for her new adventure, Mordecai gave her some important advice. He suggested to Esther that she should not say anything to anyone about being Jewish. Esther, excited about what lay ahead of her, readily agreed.

The selection process from this point on is really quite interesting. The young women who were selected to participate in this process were put through the rigors of twelve months of beauty treatments—including six months of being treated with oil of myrrh and six months with perfumes and cosmetics.

All of this was necessary before they were presented to King Xerxes. Here is what is both fascinating and disturbing: All this lavish attention was poured out on them to prepare them to spend *one night* with the King. Just one night. After the one night, they were sent to a second harem where they were to remain until the King called for them by name. For a year, someone has noted, these girls had been moisturizing their skin, putting on perfume, doing their hair, etc.—and for what? In truth, a one-night stand. If the King did not call for them they would never, ever return to his side. One scholar estimates that somewhere between 400 and 1,400 girls took their turn along with Esther in seeking the King's approval.

Now you might be thinking that the Bible's description of this selection process is exaggerated. All those young virgins and all that beautification—surely the writer got carried away. Not so. In fact there was a report on CNN as recently as 2005 that in the small African nation of Swaziland more than 50,000 young women were participating in that year's annual Reed Dance, a ritual instituted so that the king of Swaziland could choose a new bride.

King Mswati III, who already has twelve wives, was criticized for establishing a ritual like the Reed Dance in a nation where women's roles are changing, but that did not keep the event from being held.

The young women who participated in the Reed Dance were required to be virgins. In this case, they spent one week before the ceremony undergoing beauty rituals. Many young women in this impoverished nation dream of being the king's wife because of the luxury and security that such a post guarantees. There are rumors that each of the king's wives has her own house and a BMW. A really fortunate royal wife may one day be granted status as the Queen Mother, in which case she would earn the title "Great She-Elephant." [32]

We don't know if the Queen of Persia was fortunate enough to carry a title like "Great She-Elephant," but we can assume there were some perks associated with marrying the king.

This was the routine that Esther became part of. At the beginning she entered the royal harem under the supervision of a servant of the King named Hegai. It wasn't long before Esther became Hegai's favorite. To increase her chances of catching the King's eye, Hegai ordered intensive beauty treatments and special food as well as seven female attendants to assure that she would look her best when her big moment came.

Can you imagine both the eagerness and also the hesitation

with which Esther anticipated her one big night with the King? Surely she sought out information from her fellow beauty contestants about what the King expected out of them. And surely she wanted some insight into what the King was like.

We don't know how long Esther had to wait, but finally it was her turn to spend that fateful night with Xerxes. Need I tell you that he was totally smitten by her? None of the other young women compared. And so it came to pass that Xerxes placed a royal crown on Esther's head and she became the new Queen.

Meanwhile cousin Mordecai was biding his time making certain that Esther was being well taken care of. Each day he spent time sitting at a gate at the entrance to the palace observing and listening to the chatter surrounding the palace. It is amazing what you hear when you are focused on what goes on around you. Anxiously wanting to hear any news about his cousin, one day Mordecai heard two of the king's officers making plans to assassinate Xerxes! He immediately sent word to Esther who told the King about this plot, thereby sparing his life. She gave credit to Mordecai for passing on this critical information.

When the charge was investigated and found true, the two officers were hanged on a gallows. A record of this event was entered into the King's logbook and then promptly forgotten. However, this event becomes important later on in our story, so hold on to it.

Xerxes and Esther should have lived happily ever after, but remember there is a villain in our story, the vain and pompous man named Haman. Haman was the second highest-ranking official in the empire after the King. And remember, Haman's vanity knew no bounds.

For example, there was a law that everyone in the kingdom should bow to Haman as the second-in-command just as they would to the King himself. And Haman relished this law. In fact, he would ride through the streets of the city on a regular basis just to experience this overt display of the people's forced devotion. It gave him great pleasure to see all the people bow as he passed by. Indeed, the firing of the endorphins in his brain as he watched them bow was probably comparable to a drug addict experiencing the high of being injected with an illicit drug. He needed the adulation to make his life complete.

Everyone bowed down to Haman except for one stubborn Jewish man named . . . you guessed it . . . Mordecai, Queen Esther's cousin. Mordecai's deep Jewish faith would not allow him to bow to anyone but God. This infuriated Haman. It infuriated him to the extent that he vowed not only to eliminate Mordecai but all Jews throughout the kingdom.

Haman was so resolute to carry out this evil plan that he designated a special day on which these pesky people would be slain—the thirteenth day of the twelfth month which was called the month of Adar. For some reason Haman selected this day by casting lots or "purs" as they were called in the language of the time. To this day, the Jewish celebration associated with the story of Esther is called "Purim" to commemorate the casting of lots, or purs, in this plot to commit genocide against the Jewish people. The Jews have been persecuted many times in their history. There is a saying in the Jewish community: "There are so many Hamans, but only one Purim."

Haman approached King Xerxes with his sinister plan. He explained that the entire empire was threatened by a certain group of people who disregarded the king's laws. He was speaking, of course, of the Jews. Haman even offered to finance their annihilation by contributing to the royal treasury 375 tons of his own silver.

King Xerxes told him he could keep his money, but he could do whatever he wanted with those people he considered a threat. It was not King Xerxes' finest hour. Perhaps he was so enraptured with Esther that he left his more critical ruling judgments to others. After all, to this point, he has no idea that Esther is Jewish and that his decree will also apply to her.

And thus the decree was sent out that on the appointed day all Jews—men, women and children—would be put to death. The Nazis were not the first people in history to propose the annihilation of the Jewish people.

When Mordecai learned about this horrendous decree, he ripped his clothes to shreds and put on sackcloth and ashes and went out into the streets wailing bitterly. Esther learned of her cousin's behavior and was shocked. Living cloistered in the palace Esther obviously had no idea that this decree threatening her people had been issued. All she could think of was how embarrassing Mordecai's behavior was. She immediately sent out new clothes to him, but he wouldn't accept them.

Instead, Mordecai sent word to her about the catastrophic

decree. He somehow omitted telling her that this decree came about partly because of his own stubbornness in angering Haman. However, he pleaded for her to intervene with King Xerxes before it was too late.

This presented a dilemma for Esther. There was a law that anyone who approached the King without being summoned could be put to death—unless he extended his golden scepter to them and thereby spared their life. This law applied to the Queen just as it did to the ordinary citizen. It had been thirty days since the King had asked for Esther. She sent word to Mordecai that what he was asking of her was simply impossible under the circumstances. She could, after all, be put to death.

It was time that Esther had a wake-up call in language Mordecai had never used with her before. She needed to know that her life was already in jeopardy, but not only her life, but the life of all their people as well. It is within this context that Mordecai sent Esther a message that is one of the most famous and most meaningful passages in the Bible: "Do not think that because you are in the king's house that you alone of all the Jews will escape. For if you remain silent at this time, relief and deliverance for the Jews will arise from another place but you and your father's family will perish. And who knows whether you have not come to the kingdom for such a time as this?"

In other words Mordecai was saying to her, "Esther, your life is already in danger. And how do you know whether God has put you in your present position just so you can intervene and save your people?"

It is a powerful question, isn't it? It's a question we should ask ourselves from time to time. How do we know that God hasn't placed us where we are so we can make a difference in someone's life? How do we know whether God has not brought us to this place in our lives so that we can make a difference in the world?

This is an extraordinary statement of faith about your role and mine in the Kingdom of God. It reminds me of an old folk legend which says that scattered throughout the earth, there are twenty-eight people on whom the future of the world depends. These twenty-eight people do not know who they are, but their actions determine whether the world will continue or not. You and I could be among those upon whom the world depends. "And who knows whether you have not come to the kingdom for such a time as this?"

Fortunately Esther was moved into action by Mordecai's blunt wake-up message. And at this critical juncture in her life we begin to see that Esther was not only beautiful but courageous as well. Perhaps at this moment she awoke to the reality of God's presence in her life, even though she does not mention God's name. Perhaps it occurred to her that it was not ultimately her doing that put her in this royal position. There were many other beautiful women that the King had at his disposal. Perhaps there was another reason he had selected her to be his Queen, something over which she had no control.

Whatever her reasoning, Esther sent her cousin Mordecai a remarkable and courageous return message: "Go, gather together all the Jews who are in Susa and fast for me. Do not eat or drink for three days, night or day. I and my attendants will fast as you do. When this is done, I will go to the king, even though it is against the law. If I perish, I perish."

Those too are memorable words: "If I perish, I perish." Esther was proving that she was as beautiful on the inside as she was on the outside. Literally, we see that there was more to Esther than meets the eye.

Three days later Esther approached King Xerxes. Fortunately the King extended the golden scepter which signaled approval of her action. "What is your desire?" he asked. "Ask and it's yours, even if it's half my kingdom!"

"If it pleases the king," said Esther, "let the king and Haman attend a dinner tomorrow I will prepare."

The next day both the King and Haman arrived at Esther's quarters for the dinner she had arranged. In time Xerxes asked her the important question, "Now what is it that you want Esther? You may have half of my kingdom if you desire it, just ask."

For some unknown reason, Esther still wasn't prepared to make her request. She answered, "I would like for you and Haman to again come tomorrow for dinner and it will be then that I will make my request."

Haman, quite full of himself as usual, was very pleased to be invited for a return visit to the Queen's quarters. However, as he was leaving the palace his eye fell on Mordecai sitting outside at the main gate. As usual Mordecai refused to bow down to Haman and, in fact, totally ignored him. Haman was irate.

Later that evening Haman was typically braggadocios in telling his wife and some friends about how much money he had and about his high position in the King's government. He regaled them with the story of his private dinner with the King and Queen and the fact that he was returning for another dinner the next day. Then Haman, in the middle of his ostentatious brag-fest, paused and confessed sadly that he couldn't enjoy any of his success as long as that Jew who sat at the palace gate refused to bow to him.

His wife and friends offered a suggestion. "Haman," they said, "why not build a gallows, a big one seventy-five feet high and have Mordecai hanged on it. Then you can go to dinner with the King and Queen and have a really good time."

What an excellent suggestion, thought Haman. And so the next morning construction was begun on a huge gallows.

During the night, even as Haman was lying in bed contemplating the building of the gallows for Mordecai, King Xerxes was having a fitful night's sleep. Finally, he gave up on slumbering. In order to pass the time he ordered the logbook of his reign to be brought to him for review. As he read the logbook he was reminded of the plot to assassinate him by his two officers. And he was reminded of Mordecai's role in saving his life. He wondered what honors were ever bestowed on Mordecai for this great service to the King. When he learned nothing had yet been done, he decided to ask Haman's advice.

The next morning he summoned Haman to his quarters. "Haman," he asked, what would be an appropriate gesture for a man that the king especially wants to honor?"

Egotistically, Haman thought to himself, "Who would the king want to honor but me?" So he said to the king, "Have them bring a royal robe which the king has worn and a horse the king has ridden, one with a royal crest. Then let one of the king's most noble princes robe the man you wish to honor and lead him on the horse through the city streets, proclaiming before him, 'This is the man the king delights to honor!'"

"A most perfect and wonderful idea," said King Xerxes. "I want you to take the robe and horse and do what you have proposed for Mordecai the Jew who sits outside the palace gate. Don't leave out a single detail of your plan."

And so Haman spent the rest of his day living out his worst nightmare. He took the robe and horse and led Mordecai through the city square, proclaiming before him, "This is the man the king delights to honor! This is the man the king delights to honor." This was the worst day in Haman's life. Well not quite. A worse day is yet to come.

That evening the King and Haman returned to Esther's quarters for dinner. Haman wanted to enjoy this night, knowing that soon Mordecai would hang from the tall gallows he was having constructed. The act of leading the horse with Mordecai on it through the city streets and announcing that Mordecai was being honored by the king was more than Haman could endure. But soon he would have his revenge.

In the Queen's quarters they were soon eating and drinking again and the humiliating events of the day were receding slowly from Haman's brain. Finally King Xerxes asked the Queen the question that had prompted this second evening's festivities. "Esther, what would you like? Half of my kingdom! Just ask and it's yours."

Esther answered, "If I have found favor with you, Your Majesty, and if it pleases you, grant me my life, this is my petition. Spare my people, this is my request. For I and my people have been sold to be annihilated."

King Xerxes exploded. "Who is responsible for this?" he asked with fury.

Esther replied, "This evil man, Haman." Suddenly Haman was terrified.

King Xerxes, full of rage, left his wine and stalked out into the palace garden. Haman was left to plead with Queen Esther for his life.

Just as the king returned from the garden, Haman, who had too much to drink, bending over the Queen to plead his case, fell on the couch where Esther was reclining. The king roared. "Will he even molest the queen while she is with me in my house?"

All the blood drained from Haman's face. Haman was finished and he knew it. In an ironic turn of events, Haman was hanged on the seventy-five foot high gallows that he had built for Mordecai. King Xerxes gave Queen Esther Haman's estate. And, to add insult to injury, he gave Mordecai Haman's position as second-in-command in the empire.

In the days that followed as depicted in the last chapter of Esther, there is much violence as cousins Esther and Mordecai eliminate the rest of the enemies of the Jewish people—but let's try not to think about that. I want to visualize them singing and dancing at the end of my Broadway musical.

Now how did this little romantic melodrama that doesn't even mention the name of God make it into the Holy Scriptures?

Old Testament scholar Walter Brueggemann suggests that the book of Esther is there to inspire an oppressed people to keep going, to keep looking for ways to bounce back, to challenge the powers that threaten to overwhelm, not to give up.

That is certainly a valid explanation. But I would like to think this little book is in the Scriptures also to inspire us with the story of a young woman who grew in her role as the Queen of an empire. Think of her situation. She was in her exalted position only because of her good looks. But there was far more to her than that. She was a person who loved her guardian and loved her people and ultimately, loved God.

She lived in a very restrictive situation. She didn't have any real personal intimacy with her husband. She could not even go talk with him without prior approval. She didn't have any power over her own life. She didn't have any security in the face of those who planned to kill her and her people. And yet, when the time came that she could make a difference—saving her people from certain genocide—she stepped up and did her part.

On a smaller scale, you and I are tested at times in our life to take a stand that will make a difference in someone's life, perhaps a difference in our community, or even a difference in the world as a whole. Will we do our part? I hope so.

In the words of the wise and devout man Mordecai, "Who knows whether you have come to the kingdom for such a time as this?"

HOSEA AND GOMER
Hosea 1-14

If there had been an ancient version of the *Jerry Springer Show*, you can bet that our next couple would have been featured guests. The little book of Hosea contains a fascinating love story, a different kind of love story: it involves a man of God, Hosea, who marries a prostitute named Gomer.

Hosea went into his relationship with Gomer with his eyes wide open. It wasn't as if she misled him. He knew what she was like when he married her. She had been a harlot. Marriage changed her very little. Isn't that the way it normally works? Conversion changes people, marriage rarely does.

The situation between Hosea and Gomer was the exact opposite from the old truism: *A man marries a woman expecting that she will not change, but she does. A woman marries a man expecting that he will change, but he doesn't.* Hosea married Gomer hoping she would change, but she didn't.

It may be that Gomer was a temple prostitute in the service of the Canaanite fertility god, Baal. This temple employed both male and female prostitutes. Regardless of whether she was a temple prostitute or an ordinary harlot, it is clear that Gomer entered this lifestyle willingly. So it is shocking that Hosea would be involved with her at all. And then to marry her and to try and turn her into a model wife and mother—what was he thinking? He failed miserably, of course. But out of his experience, Hosea gained new insights into the love of God for sinful people like you and me.

Hosea's story begins about seven or eight hundred years before Christ. Hosea was the last great prophet of the Northern Kingdom (Israel). He was a contemporary of the prophet Amos, whose ministry was to the Southern Kingdom (Judah). Amos was the stereotypical prophet of doom and gloom. Think John the Baptist. Hosea was a more compassionate witness. Think Jesus. In fact, Hosea's name means "salvation." It is derived from the same root word as the names Joshua and Jesus. While the name of Jesus, of course, stands above all names, it might be helpful to think for a moment of these three names together. Jesus is the New Testament's Joshua, leading humanity to the new Promised Land. Hosea is the Old Testament's preacher of grace, one who prefigures the message of Christ.

Hosea lived during a time of much political and spiritual turmoil, a time when the country was financially wealthy, but morally bankrupt. It is difficult to speak on behalf of God when times are bad; it is even more difficult when times are good. People watch their stock portfolios soar and think to themselves, "We must be doing something right," even when they are living shoddy lives that bring God no glory.

Even the priests were guilty of neglecting their religious duties and leading people astray. Meanwhile the people were drawn to Baal, the fertility god. They had forgotten how God had fed them in the wilderness. Now they were looking to Baal to bless their crops. Besides, the worship of Baal was more fun. I shudder to think what might happen if competing religions in our land offered inducements like temple prostitutes. And so the people were letting their relationship with Yahweh, the one true God, slide. Hosea could see in his relationship with Gomer the pain that Israel's unfaithfulness brought God.

Three children are produced from the union of Hosea and Gomer—Jezreel, Lo-ruhamah, and Lo-ammi. The children's names have symbolic value; they reflect the turmoil in Hosea and Gomer's marriage. Jezreel was the name of one son, which means "I will scatter." It is also the name of a valley where a terrible battle took place. Lo-ruhamah was their daughter. Tragically, her name means "not loved." Lo-ammi is the name of another son. His name means "not mine." As you can guess from their names, Hosea was probably not the father of the latter two children.

What an unhappy home. Two children of questionable paternity with names like "not loved" and "not mine." A wife and mother who has not escaped her past as a prostitute, still seducing every man in sight. And a husband and father trying desperately to hold his family together.

And then Gomer leaves. Our thought is, good riddance. She's done enough damage. But that's not Hosea's reaction. Hosea can't get Gomer out of his mind and out of his heart. Even after he discovers that she has gone back to her life as a prostitute, he pursues her. When he finds her, she is being sold on an auction block like a head of cattle.

There she stands, in public, stark naked. The men in the crowd are leering at her and preparing to bid. We know from earlier references in the Hebrew Bible the shame and scandal associated with nakedness.

Hosea takes all this in and his poor heart is broken. He knows he should walk away. She's made her bed; let her lie in it. Any other man would have called it quits right there, but not Hosea. When the time comes and the auctioneer calls out Gomer's number, who steps up with the winning bid but Hosea? He buys his unfaithful wife back for fifteen pieces of silver and ten bushels of barley. What a remarkable act. She could have been stoned to death for the life style she had chosen. By Old Testament standards that is what she deserved. But Hosea loved her with a love big enough to forgive. So Hosea bought her back. This man, whose name means "salvation," could not know that a few hundred years later, a man named Jesus, a named derived from the same root word as his name, would buy back unfaithful humanity from sin and death.

And then a light bulb switches on in Hosea's brain: his love for Gomer is a pale reflection of God's love for God's unfaithful people. This is a remarkable breakthrough in Old Testament thinking. In verse 6:4 we read of that love when God speaks through Hosea and asks, "O Ephraim, what shall I do with you? O Judah what shall I do with you? . . ."

Christine Wicker left the church sometime in college. There were many reasons for her disenchantment, chiefly that she didn't feel that the church answered any of her questions about God. For years, she ignored or denied the idea of God. But Wicker came back to God in a surprising way. After a string of bad relationships, Wicker married a man named Philip. And it was Philip's unconditional, trustworthy, accepting love that broke through to her. As she would write in her book *God Knows My Heart,* "I didn't connect this love with God. Not at first. But it was miraculous to me, and as the years went by, I began to think that if a person could love me with such openness, then maybe God could, too. If there is a God, and if He does love people, I began to ask, what would His love be like? Would it be less than the love my husband shows to me?" [27]

This is a message of Grace. God's love exceeds His people's vilest sins. God is not interested in punishing Israel, but in saving her, loving her, and making her His own.

It shocks us to think that Hosea could love this kind of woman, but isn't that the point? Paul writes about God's love for humanity in Romans 5:7-8: "Very rarely will anyone die for a righteous man, though for a good man someone might possibly dare to die. But God demonstrates his own love for us in this: While we were still sinners, Christ died for us."

This is a message that you and I depend on. God loves us, even when we are unlovable, unfaithful, indifferent. God is always calling us home. Anyone who says that the God of the Old Testament is a God of wrath while the God of the New Testament is a God of love has never read the book of Hosea. The judgment of God is there all right, but it is always a judgment tempered by a love that cannot let go.

Now I must tell you that there is another less romantic approach we might take to the story of Hosea. This approach states that Hosea's act of taking Gomer as his wife was a symbolic act directed by God—not an act of romantic love. Certainly the text directs us toward that verdict: "When the Lord began to speak through Hosea, the Lord said to him, 'Go, take to yourself an adulterous wife and children of unfaithfulness, because the land is guilty of the vilest adultery in departing from the Lord.'" (1:2)

That is why Hosea married a prostitute: according to this interpretation, God told him to. God wanted to dramatize to the people just how unhappy God was with Israel's adulterous behavior with the god Baal, so God instructed His prophet to marry a harlot as an object lesson. The message of Hosea's book is still the same—the message of God's faithful love for unfaithful people—but Hosea didn't really love Gomer according to this interpretation, he was just obeying God.

This interpretation of Hosea's story has many precedents. Old Testament prophets were notorious for their symbolic acts. Isaiah walked naked and barefoot through the streets of Jerusalem. Jeremiah shattered pottery as people came into the temple. And Ezekiel lay on his left side for 390 days and on his right side for 40 days and shaved his head with a sword. In the same way God told Hosea to take a prostitute for a wife simply and solely to dramatize God's judgment of as well as God's love for Israel.

If we look at the story as a series of symbolic acts then, in chapter one we see God telling Hosea to take this prostitute as a wife in the same way that God took a group of people worshiping a calf out in the wilderness and molded them into His people. Then, in chapter two, we see God divorcing this same people for their unfaithfulness by sending them into exile. That happened to Israel in Hosea's lifetime. Israel entered into a treaty with Assyria in the hopes of gaining some security, instead of trusting God for their security. But Assyria turned on Israel and in 722 B.C. destroyed the land. All the members of the upper classes and many of the ordinary people were taken captive and carried off to live as prisoners of war.

Finally, in chapter three we see God pursuing His unfaithful people, just as Hosea pursued Gomer, and restoring them after the exile.

In each of these chapters we see a struggle going on between God's judgment and God's love. Chapter one, in which God instructs Hosea to marry this prostitute, ends with these words, "Yet the Israelites will be like the sand on the seashore, which cannot be measured or counted. In the place where it was said to them, 'You are not my people,' they will be called 'sons of the living God.' The people of Judah and the people of Israel will be reunited, and they will appoint one leader and will come up out of the land, for great will be the day of Jezreel."

Chapter two contains bitter words about Israel's sins, but closes with these words: "In that day," declares the LORD, "you will call me 'my husband'; you will no longer call me 'my master . . . I will betroth you to me forever; I will betroth you in righteousness and justice, in love and compassion. I will betroth you in faithfulness, and you will acknowledge the LORD . . . I will show my love to the one I called 'Not my loved one.' I will say to those called 'Not my people,' 'You are my people'; and they will say, 'You are my God.'"

And chapter three closes with an affirmation that Israel shall be restored as God's people. A struggle is going on within every chapter, a struggle between God's judgment and God's grace.

Singer Steven Curtis Chapman was speaking of the New Testament when he made this comment, but it applies equally well to the God revealed in the Hebrew Bible, especially the God revealed in the book of Hosea. He said, "In the Gospel, we discover we are far worse off than we thought, and far more loved than we ever dreamed."

So, does the story of Hosea and Gomer reflect mere symbolic act or sincere love? The plain meaning of the text suggests the former. However, life experience suggests the latter. I guess it comes down to how you think God spoke to people in biblical times. Did God speak to them with a voice they could hear with their physical ears, or did God speak to them through their experiences, much like God speaks to us today? We can only guess. Perhaps the prophets took direct dictation from God.

However, Hosea would not be the first or the last preacher who would speak about God from his personal experience. Is it not possible that, as Hosea looked back over his life, he could see God's hand at work? Suddenly he realized that God led him into his union with Gomer in order to teach him a bigger lesson about love and grace. That happens, doesn't it? At any one point in life we may not be sure what God's will for us is. But as we look back over our lives, we begin to see that God was there all the time.

As for the struggle between judgment and grace, it is certainly God's most difficult conundrum. God gives us freedom, including the freedom to destroy ourselves. However, it grieves God when we misuse our freedom. Why? Because it hurts God? No, because it hurts us, God's beloved. So there is a struggle, a struggle epitomized by the cross of Christ. Salvation from sin is serious business because sin destroys people.

Let's use a parable. In his book *A View from the Zoo*, Gary Richmond, a former zoo keeper, tells about a young friend of his named Julie who owned a raccoon. Raccoons are gentle creatures when they are young, but they go through a glandular change at about 24 months. After that, they often attack their owners. A 30-pound raccoon can be equal to a 100-pound dog in a scrap. Richmond felt compelled to warn Julie of the change coming to her pet raccoon, Bandit. She listened politely, then responded by saying what people always say, "It will be different for me . . ." And she smiled as she added, "Bandit wouldn't hurt me. He just wouldn't."

Three months later Julie underwent plastic surgery for facial lacerations sustained when Bandit attacked her for no apparent reason. [28]

"It will be different for me . . ." Does any young person who begins experimenting with alcohol or drugs ever expect that he or she will get hooked? Does any married person who becomes involved in an extra-marital affair ever look down the road to see the destruction he or she is bringing to other people involved?

"It will be different for me . . .," but it never is. God hates sin because of what it does to people.

So, there is a struggle between God's judgment and God's grace. But God's grace always wins. Even if Hosea had to pursue Gomer to the end of the earth, he would have done it. That is the nature of pure love. Maybe I am being overly romantic and sentimental, but that is how I see this love story. It is a story of true love that reveals an even more magnificent love, the love of God.

This does not mean that God does not deal harshly at times with His people. Sometimes the only voice we hear is one of reprimand. And a reprimand can be an expression of love, just as much as a hug can be. We shout "stop" to our child as she heads for the busy highway. We may even give a little smack to the hands that try to stick an object into an electrical outlet. It is not because we enjoy exerting our authority. It is because of our great love for that child, a love that will never cease. So God is sometimes harsh with us, but for a reason. He has established a covenant relationship with us. Anything that endangers that relationship will not be tolerated.

Pastor Lawrence O. Richards writes, "There's a vast difference between the 'I love you's' breathlessly exchanged in the back seat of a car, and the 'I do's' shared at a wedding! [People] think that if they make a few token sacrifices to God, then He will forgive them and restore their society. But God is calling for deep, heartfelt repentance and the end of all idolatry before He will forgive . . ." [29]

Speaking of children, there is another beautiful image in Hosea that prefigures the teaching of Jesus. God is likened not only to a husband pursuing an unfaithful wife, but God is also likened to a loving parent. We read in chapter 11: "When Israel was a child, I loved him and out of Egypt I called my son. The more I called them, the more they went from me . . . Yet it was I who taught Ephraim to walk, I took them up in my arms . . . ." (1-3a)

This is a more familiar image to us—God as a father teaching His child—slowly, tenderly—how to walk. It is not very far from the God of Hosea to the God Jesus revealed to us when he taught us to pray, "Abba". . . "Daddy."

Jay Bakker, son of former televangelist Jim Bakker, now leads a ministry for teens in Atlanta, Georgia. He says that he never heard messages of God's love and grace in his childhood church. He grew up believing that God was just waiting to catch him in his sins and to condemn him. He remembers his father's first church. On the church wall was a painting of a giant eye. This eye represented the all-seeing, all-knowing nature of God. To Jay, the eye symbolized God's constant judgment on him. He was scared to death of not living up to God's standards, of not being holy enough to earn God's love.

After Jay's father, Jim, faced scandal and disgrace in his own ministry, Jay became even more convinced of God's judgment on sinners. Christian friends and colleagues turned their back on the Bakker family. They became the butt of jokes in Christian circles. Once again, Jay felt like a failure in God's eyes. But Jay saw a transformation take place in his father's life after Jim was sentenced to prison. In prison, Jim Bakker experienced God's overwhelming love and presence and peace. He realized what God's grace is all about. He was able to let go of his past, and to forgive those who turned their backs on him. Through his father's changed life, and through the love and acceptance of a few kind Christians, Jay writes, "I discovered the shocking secret: God loves me just the way I am." [30]

This is the simple, yet life-changing, message of Hosea: God loves you just the way you are. No wonder Hosea is quoted so often in the New Testament. Jesus refers to him, as does St. Paul. Hosea 13:14 states that someday God will destroy Death. Some scholars believe that 1 Corinthians 15:55, "O Death, where is your sting? O Hades, where is your victory?" is a reference to this verse.

Seven or eight hundred years before Christ, God was seeking to reveal to His people the path of grace. Not a cheap grace in which sin is ignored, but a very expensive grace in which God pursues His unfaithful people and pays any price to bring that people home. We said in the introduction to this book that there is only one truly great love story in Scripture and this is it: God's love for unfaithful and unfit humanity. Thank God for that love. It is our only hope.

ELIZABETH AND ZECHARIAH
Luke 1

Years ago I read a book titled *Barren Couples and Broken Hearts*. It is about married couples who desperately want to have children but who, for one reason or another, are unable.

It is one of life's ironies, isn't it? Some couples have unexpected and even unwanted pregnancies. Other couples who are totally unfit to be parents also have no difficulty breeding. Then there are those couples who have so much love to give that they would probably make wonderful parents, but are denied the opportunity.

Not everyone in our society wants to be a parent. That's okay. No one should ever be made to feel unworthy because they make this choice. But there are some couples who want desperately to have children. Often these are some of the best people in the world. They are able both financially and emotionally to be the very best of parents, but nature does not cooperate. Some will choose adoption. Others will choose to focus on each other and accept their childless state.

Elizabeth and Zechariah fit in this category. They were an older couple and, like Abraham and Sarah, they had no children. Zechariah was a priest of the tribe of Levi (you remember —Leah's boy). Zechariah's name means "Yahweh remembers." We don't know exactly where Zechariah and Elizabeth lived. Luke just tells us that it was a "town in the hill country of Judea."

The Bible describes Zechariah and his wife Elizabeth as

"righteous before God, living blamelessly according to all the commandments and regulations of the Lord." According to Jewish law and custom, priests were to marry virgins of Israelite birth. Elizabeth was undoubtedly a virgin when she married Zechariah, and she was also of the tribe of Levi. So she was also from the priestly tradition, perhaps a "preacher's kid" herself. A match made in heaven, you would think.

Except for one thing—they had no children. They were a devoted couple—devoted to God and to one another, but they did not have the joy of having a little one running around the house. They had reached the age where such a thing was unrealistic. They had learned to cope with it. God knew best, they believed.

Still, their pain was real. In biblical times, an inability to have children was regarded as a tragedy, a disgrace and even a sign of God's punishment. Children were understood to be blessings from God for three important reasons: children carry on the family name; children perpetuate God's covenant with Israel; and children provide care for their parents in old age.

So, like most couples in their situation in biblical times, the lack of a child in their home was a very big disappointment to Zechariah and Elizabeth. But what could they do? They couldn't do anything, but God could.

It came time for Zechariah to take his turn serving at the temple in Jerusalem. On the day in question, Zechariah "was chosen by lot . . . to enter the sanctuary of the Lord and offer incense." For Zechariah, this was a once-in-a-lifetime opportunity, for to be in the sanctuary of the Lord, was to be in the very presence of God.

There Zechariah was—burning incense while a great multitude of people were praying outside. At that moment, an angel appeared to him on the right side of the altar, and it frightened Zechariah. Have you ever noticed that, whenever people in the Bible meet angels, the first thing the angel says is, "Don't be afraid." Evidently meeting an angel is an unsettling experience.

Gabriel said to Zechariah, "Don't be afraid. Your prayer has been heard. Your wife Elizabeth will bear you a son, and you shall call his name John." Then the angel Gabriel went on to say that John would be a great man, full of the Holy Spirit from the day of his birth. "He will turn many of the children of Israel to the Lord their God," said the angel.

Then the angel said something even more extraordinary: their child was to be the long-awaited messenger who would announce the coming of the Messiah. Their son would be the messenger described in the Old Testament book of Malachi. Malachi told the people of a future prophet when he proclaimed, "I will send my messenger to prepare the way for me." (Mal. 3:1) John the Baptist was that messenger sent by God to prepare the people for the coming of the Messiah. This was an extraordinary message that the angel brought to Zechariah.

Evidently Zechariah was a man who accepted very few things on faith—he had to be shown, so he asked for a sign: "How shall I know this," Zechariah said, "for I am an old man and my wife is advanced in years."

Let me make a suggestion to you. If an angel appears to you and gives you some news, don't question it. Zechariah asked for a sign and he got a sign. Gabriel told Zechariah that he would be speechless until these things came about!

So, there was poor Zechariah in the temple—it was his duty to come out of the temple and bless the people waiting on the outside—but he couldn't speak! And furthermore, he was late, very late, coming out of the temple as well!

When he did come out, everyone knew something important had happened in the temple. They realized that the old priest had seen a vision. When the preacher is struck speechless in church, he surely has been in the presence of God.

Zechariah tried to communicate with the people who had been waiting on him by making signs with his hands. Can you imagine the scene when he got home? I would have liked to have seen him pantomime to Elizabeth that, in her advanced years, she would conceive and bear a child. They would have a son and he would grow up to be a very special man. It was probably a hilarious scene. But it was also a sobering scenario. That night they surely clung to one another in joy and disbelief.

Everything happened of course just as the angel said it would. Elizabeth became pregnant. She was so filled with joy that she sang out, "Now at last the Lord has helped me."

You might have thought that God would have chosen someone

else besides Elizabeth and Zechariah to be the parents of John the Baptist. After all, he was the chosen one who would prepare the people of Israel for the coming of the Messiah. God might have chosen a younger, more energetic couple for this task. God is full of surprises. What God is looking for is not external circumstance. All God looks for is faith.

Elizabeth stayed in seclusion for about 5 months while she awaited the birth of her child. Perhaps she was slightly embarrassed. Certainly she was in no hurry to draw attention to her condition. All her friends were grandmothers and she was preparing to have her first child. It was all too much.

Now you may wonder how life was for Elizabeth during this time of waiting, especially with Zechariah unable to talk. It was probably kind of nice. Being a priest, Zechariah was probably a bit tedious to listen to at times. Here Elizabeth was going through a pregnancy late in life—and she had a husband who could only listen to her. He couldn't interrupt, he couldn't argue. He couldn't preach or offer solutions. All he could do was listen and write notes. Elizabeth probably enjoyed those notes.

Then the story grows even more dramatic.

Elizabeth did not know that the same angel who appeared to Zechariah had also appeared to a relative of hers—a much younger woman betrothed to a carpenter named Joseph. Elizabeth learned of Mary's pregnancy in the six month of her own pregnancy, when one day out of the blue, Mary knocked on her door.

In spite of the difference in their ages, Mary and Elizabeth were evidently very close, for as soon as Gabriel told Mary that she, too, was to bear a very special child, a child that would save his people, Mary grabbed up her things and headed to visit Elizabeth and Zechariah. This was no leisurely stroll. We're told that the hill country between Nazareth and the place where Elizabeth lived was rather bleak. "The eastern slopes were mostly impassable desert, stretching 10 to 15 miles from their highest point, 3000 feet near Hebron, down to the Dead Sea, the lowest point on earth at 1,300 feet below sea level. The vast wasteland was broken only by imposing cliffs and canyons and a few forts and oases . . . It was an area fit for fugitives, rebels, and hermits, but certainly not for a pregnant woman." [33]

Some scholars believe the journey was something on the order of seventy-five miles—on foot. Given the difficulties and dangers that the landscape posed, it was obviously very important to Mary to share her own mind-boggling news with Elizabeth. And so, with the impetuousness of youth she made the journey.

Now she stood at Elizabeth's door. And Luke tells us something very special about that encounter. He says, "The babe leaped in [Elizabeth's] womb and Elizabeth was filled with the Holy Spirit, and she exclaimed [to Mary], 'Blessed are you among women, and blessed is the child you will bear!'"

Isn't that interesting? A six-month-pregnant "mature" woman named Elizabeth was the first person in the New Testament to announce the coming of Christ. And after she makes this announcement, she says something else quite significant: "But why am I so favored, that the mother of my Lord should come to me? As soon as the sound of your greeting reached my ears, the baby in my womb leaped for joy. Blessed is **she who has believed** that the Lord would fulfill his promises to her (emphasis added)!"

This is one of the few times that a feminine pronoun is used with a blessing in the Bible. Almost universally we read, "Blessed is he . . ." but not here. We read, "Blessed is **she who has believed** that what the Lord has said to her will be accomplished!"

This passage taken from the story of the first Christmas elevates women beyond anything found in the Bible. Let the literalists argue that the rib taken from man's side in the Genesis story consigns woman to a secondary role. We will take them to Bethlehem and show them the Son of God born of a woman. And we will show them an older woman, also to bear a son, who is the first to announce the coming of the Messiah. This was thirty years before her famous son, John, makes that announcement out in the wilderness.

In fact, if you accept the doctrine of the virgin birth, a man played absolutely no role and had no part in our Lord's birth. Only God and a young woman named Mary. Yet even today there are people who thump their Bibles and insist that woman is supposed to be subservient to man.

People get the strangest ideas about what the Bible teaches. If we were to stop right here with this story of Mary and Elizabeth, we would say that woman, not man, was favored by God. However, what is clear is that the Bible teaches that neither gender is superior. We're not saved by the shape of our flesh, but by the sureness of our faith!

What has gender got to do with it? Nothing. Absolutely nothing. God loves little boys and little girls the same. But still, this is one passage in which woman is definitely in the superior role.

People are so amazing. I heard about an old guy years ago who was convinced that all women were bad drivers. He would growl as a car cut into his lane, "Another woman driver!"

If he happened to pull up beside the offending vehicle and observe that it was a man at the wheel, he would growl, "No doubt his mother taught him to drive."

You just can't win with some people. It isn't my intention to get into the gender wars, though they are often amusing as well as infuriating.

I like comedian Elayne Boosler's definition of the difference between men and women. She says, "When women are depressed they either eat or go shopping. Men invade another country." Maybe that's not so funny after all. Maybe it is all too true.

Elizabeth, under the influence of the Holy Spirit, was the first person to identify Mary as the mother of the Messiah. When she finished, Mary launched into a song, "My soul glorifies the Lord and my spirit rejoices in God my Savior, for he has been mindful of the humble state of his servant . . ."

Elizabeth probably worried about her younger cousin. Mary was in a precarious situation. A girl not yet married and already carrying a child. Their community was strict about such things. Legally, if Joseph turned his back on her, she could be stoned to death. At the very least she would be subjected to severe humiliation. And Joseph still did not know about the impending birth. Mary stayed with Elizabeth and Zechariah for three months before going back to face the music with Joseph.

Mary was undoubtedly a blessing to this older couple as they prepared for the birth of their son. And Elizabeth surely became somewhat of a mentor to Mary. That's always been the secret strength of women, hasn't it? Women support one another. Of course, we will deal more with Mary in the next chapter.

Soon Elizabeth and Zechariah's baby was born. On the day of circumcision, eight days after his birth, it was time to name him. Friends suggested they name him Zechariah, Jr., but Elizabeth said,

"Not so; he shall be called John."

Everyone asked, "Why are you naming him John? None of your relatives are named John." Then they asked Zechariah what he would name the child, and without hesitation, Zechariah motioned for a writing tablet, and wrote, "His name is John."

Immediately, after writing this, Zechariah's mouth was opened and his tongue was set free, and he began to speak, praising God. All the neighbors were filled with awe, and throughout the hill country of Judea the story spread. "Everyone who heard this," says Luke, "wondered about it, asking, 'What then is this child going to be? For the Lord's hand was with him.'"

At this point in the story old Zechariah began to sing. It's hard for a preacher to go nine months and keep silence. Here is part of what he sang: "And you, my child, will be called a prophet of the Most High; for you will go on before the Lord to prepare the way for him, to give his people the knowledge of salvation through the forgiveness of their sins, because of the tender mercy of our God, by which the rising sun will come to us from heaven to shine on those living in darkness and in the shadow of death, to guide our feet into the path of peace."

Then Luke adds, "And the child grew and became strong in spirit; and he lived in the wilderness until he appeared publicly to Israel."

God always keeps His promises. John became a great man . . . filled with the Holy Spirit. And he did what God commanded—he prepared the way for the coming of Christ.

I'm sure that Elizabeth and Zechariah's home was filled with love and happiness. Wouldn't it be great if all children could be greeted with the enthusiasm with which Elizabeth and Zechariah greeted the birth of their son? Unfortunately many are not.

One of the great scandals of our society is the prevalence of child abuse—nearly three million cases in America each year. One child dies every 4 hours from abuse. The cost to society is staggering. Two of every three prisoners convicted of first-degree murder report childhoods of physical abuse. Eighty percent of all prostitutes report histories of sexual abuse.

If you are the product of a loving and happy home, give God thanks every day of your life. You have already received the richest blessing life can bestow. And if you have children of your own, make these years count.

If, for any reason, you did not come from a happy home, your road will be rockier. But with God's help and by God's grace you can overcome. Your greatest need will be to experience the unconditional love of God so that you can pass it on to others.

Sam Levenson tells a wonderful story about the birth of his first child. The first night home the baby would not stop crying. His wife frantically flipped through the pages of Dr. Spock to find out why babies cry and what to do about it. Since Spock's book is rather long, the baby cried a long time. Grandma was in the house, but since she had not read the books on childrearing, she was not consulted. The baby continued to cry. Finally, Grandma could be silent no longer. "Put down the book," she told her children, "and pick up the baby."

Good advice. Zechariah and Elizabeth surely gave their infant son lots of love. But they also gave him a grounding in the faith of his fathers. That is why he became a great messenger.

Elizabeth and Zechariah were selected to parent this child because of their faith in God. They were not affluent or young and beautiful. All they had was simple faith. And that's what's important. Happy families don't just happen. They are part of a package. It has to do with a commitment to God and to one another. The family that prays together generally does stay together—as trite as that may sound. Faith was important to Elizabeth and Zechariah. They trusted God and they taught their son to trust God.

Notice, however, their faith did not protect them from pain. The story does not have a happy ending. Probably Elizabeth and Zechariah did not live long enough to see their son begin his public ministry. He was known throughout the region, of course, as John the Baptist because he baptized his converts. And great multitudes came out to hear him preach. Even Jesus was baptized at his hand. He clearly did "prepare the way of the Lord."

Elizabeth and Zechariah would have been so proud.

Still, John's life was taken from him when he was still young, probably at 30 or 31. He was executed by decapitation for confronting a corrupt ruler. Let's hope that his loving and devoted parents did not live to see him die so cruelly. As an old Yiddish proverb says, "Little children disturb your sleep, big ones, your life."

To have a little baby implies a big risk. It is the risk of loss. You may perhaps know about that loss. Some parents lose children in infancy; some while a child is in his teens. Still others, after the child has reached adulthood. Regardless of when it happens, it brings indescribable pain. At such times all you can do is to believe in the God who loves you and whose care is eternal.

Elizabeth and Zechariah played a critical role in the divine drama. In some ways they were probably very ordinary people. Yet God used them in extraordinary ways. That can happen when you trust God and when you are committed to one another. And their story prepares us for our next story, the grandest love story of all the biblical narratives—the story of Mary and Joseph. [34]

MARY AND JOSEPH
Matthew 1, 2; Luke 1, 2

It is ironic that, of all of our great love stories, we have the fewest details about the most significant one for Christians. That is the story of Mary and Joseph, the parents of Jesus. Most of the information we do have is found in the first two chapters of Matthew and Luke.

In Luke, the story begins in Nazareth, a small agricultural community in the northern part of Judea with a population of about 400. Nazareth was so insignificant that, at one time, some historians and archaeologists questioned whether it had ever really existed. Nazareth was in the region of Galilee, the Appalachia of its day.

"Can anything good come out of Nazareth?" asked Nathanael in John 1:46. In New Testament times, that was a popular sentiment. It is interesting that God would choose such an insignificant spot for the birth of His son.

Our story begins with a young Jewish girl named Mary. Tradition has it that Mary's parents were Joachim and Anna, members of the tribe of Judah. They were undoubtedly devout people. Their daughter Mary showed an extraordinary acquaintance with the scriptures for one so young as we shall see later in this chapter.

According to most scholars, Mary was fourteen or fifteen years old when our story takes place, a teenager. We know that, because Mary was betrothed to a man named Joseph. The typical age for betrothal in those days was 12-13 years of age, around the time of reaching puberty. One reason for such an early age for marriage was to ensure that a girl maintained her virginity. And Mary was a virgin.

There were two words used to refer to young women in scripture: *almah*, which means young woman, and *parthenos*, which refers to a young woman who is also a virgin. The word used to describe Mary is "parthenos."

Many people have struggled with the question of whether Mary really was a virgin when Jesus was born. Some time ago, Larry King, the renowned talk show host who is Jewish, was asked whom he would like to interview if he had his pick from all of history. His answer was Jesus Christ.

The questioner paused and said, "What is the one question you would like to ask him?"

Larry King answered, "I would ask him if he indeed was virgin born, because the answer to that would define history for me."

It is interesting how much difficulty we have with the virgin birth. In a day when we have the ability to manipulate the creation of human beings through sperm banks, embryo implants, and other technological marvels, it is ironic that we deny the Creator this option for the creation of a new life. With science speeding along as it is, it may be that later generations will have no difficulty with the idea of a virgin birth at all.

The virgin birth may or may not be a big deal to you, but there was an interesting article in *McCall's* Magazine sometime back. It seems that after having two children, Fran Castro of Townsville, N.C., had a tubal ligation. She and her husband, Moe, had decided that their two daughters, Jessica and Sheree, then ages five and three, were enough. But the next year after having this birth control procedure, Fran was sitting at the dining room table when she felt something move.

"Moe, if I didn't know better," she told him. "I'd swear I just felt a baby kick."

"You know that's not possible," he replied.

That's what Fran thought—until she went to the doctor. Five months later, she gave birth to the couple's third daughter, Kristy.

Moe decided to get a vasectomy. After the procedure, he confidently told Fran, "Now there's no chance of our ever having more children."

He was right . . . for a while.

In 1993, Fran started noticing the tell-tale signs of pregnancy again.

"No, it couldn't be," she thought. Out of curiosity, she decided to buy a home pregnancy test—and was completely shocked when the result was positive.

Several months later, Fran gave birth to a healthy baby boy.

"I've never delivered a baby where the mother has had a tubal ligation and the father has had a vasectomy," said Fran's physician, James Goodwin, M.D. "The odds of both procedures failing must be astronomical." He added. "All I can say is that this baby was destined to be here."

The Castros felt that way too. In fact, they named him Destin.[35]

In their own way, the Castros were as mystified by this turn of events as were Mary and Joseph that first Christmas. But one thing is for sure—Mary and Joseph had a son that, of all children ever born, was destined to be here. It has been quoted, "The life of Jesus is bracketed by two impossibilities: a virgin's womb and an empty tomb. Jesus entered our world through a door marked 'No Entrance' and left through a door marked 'No Exit.'"

Scholars are divided over the virgin birth of Jesus, but none disagree that if God chose to do it this way, He certainly had the power. But we're getting ahead of our story.

One day an angel appeared to Mary. According to Luke 1: 28, the angel said to Mary, "Rejoice! blessed art thou among women."

When Mary saw the angel, Luke tells us, "she was troubled at his saying and cast in her mind what manner of salutation this should be."

That's not surprising. In the Bible, we have plenty of examples of angels revealing themselves to people. Usually the angels' first words are something like this: "Don't be afraid! God is with you." Fear would be a totally natural, human response to seeing a supernatural being, don't you think? But the angel's first words to Mary are not, "Don't be afraid!" Instead, the angel opens with, "Rejoice! Blessed art thou among women."

Mary **was** blessed. But, isn't it interesting how sometimes God's blessings hurt?

God blessed Abram and Sarai. We've already noted how they were asked to leave their home and family to start life over in a new land. God would make Abram the father of a mighty nation, but first he had to give up any semblance of security or status.

God blessed Jacob. But first Jacob had to wrestle with an angel. He got his blessing, but in the process he wound up with a hip knocked out of joint.

Mary was blessed, but let's face it, her pregnancy could potentially result in shame, ostracism, and the possible end of her engagement to Joseph. The problems didn't end there. Because of Jesus, Mary and Joseph would have to flee to Egypt, and later Mary would see her first-born son tortured to death. And yet, the angel was telling her she was blessed.

And she was, of course. Two thousand years later, we still talk about this young Jewish girl and her role in the world's greatest drama. No doubt she was greatly blessed. But sometimes God's blessings hurt.

The angel reassures her and tells her that she has been chosen by God to bear a child. "He will be great and will be called the Son of the Most High." (Luke 1: 32) "Most High" was a term used in both the Old and New Testament to refer to God.

Mary asks how she, as a virgin, could have a child. The angel explains that the Spirit of God will "overshadow" her.

Mary replies, "I am the Lord's servant. May it be to me as you have said."

Mary is one of the few people in the Bible who didn't try to argue with an angel of the Lord, but simply accepted what the angel told her in faithful obedience.

The word Mary uses here for "servant" is used elsewhere in the Bible to refer to a "bondservant," one who willingly chose to submit himself or herself to do the work of a master.

According to Old Testament instructions, a person who had earned their freedom but still chose, out of loyalty, to remain a servant to a particular master, pierced his or her ear with an awl. This piercing indicated that the person had freely chosen servitude to their master. This was what Mary was indicating in her reply to the angel of the Lord.[36] Mary, even at a young age, was completely obedient to God. It is no wonder she was chosen of God.

After this announcement Mary, presumably excited and scared, goes to visit her cousin, Elizabeth, in the hill country of Judea. We told the story of Elizabeth and Zachariah in the previous chapter.

This was a treacherous journey to make from where Mary lived to where Elizabeth lived, so Mary was obviously intent on seeing her cousin. You will remember with what delight Elizabeth welcomed her younger cousin and the remarkable announcement that she made, "Blessed are you among women, and blessed is the child you will bear!"

After receiving Elizabeth's affirmation, Mary breaks out into a song of praise which the Christian community calls *the Magnificat.* We said earlier that Mary showed an extraordinary acquaintance with the scriptures. When she sings her song, it is made up of images and references to scriptures from Genesis, Job, Psalms, and Isaiah. Read it as if you had never read it before and notice how remarkable it is:

"My soul glorifies the Lord and my spirit rejoices in God my Savior,
> for he has been mindful of the humble state of his servant.
> From now on all generations will call me blessed,
> for the Mighty One has done great things for me—holy is his name.
> His mercy extends to those who fear him,
> from generation to generation.
> He has performed mighty deeds with his arm;
> he has scattered those who are proud in their inmost thoughts.
> He has brought down rulers from their thrones
> but has lifted up the humble.
> He has filled the hungry with good things
> but has sent the rich away empty.
> He has helped his servant Israel,
> remembering to be merciful to Abraham and his descendants

forever, even as he said to our fathers."

This is a stunning message of liberation and hope on the lips a girl barely beyond the time of puberty. Her song is a declaration that God has not forgotten the poor and the powerless. God has given her a vision of His future justice and mercy, which would be worked out through the ministry of her son. You can see what an extraordinary girl Mary was. No wonder God chose this humble maiden to bear His son.

After about three months with Elizabeth, Mary returned home.

Now we turn to the book of Matthew which tells us about Joseph's reactions to the birth of Mary's child. It's interesting. Probably no event in history has produced as many dramatic representations as the nativity of Christ. And yet one of the main characters, Joseph, doesn't have a speaking part. Joseph doesn't say a single word in the Gospels. He listens, and he obeys. That's it and that's enough. Although Joseph came from the royal lineage of King David it is obvious he was a very humble man.

Now, how do we know he came from the royal lineage of David? It is because Matthew 1:1 begins with the genealogy of Jesus. Genealogies were important to the Jewish people for a number of reasons. They were used to establish status and legitimacy. For example, a king could show his right to rule by pointing to all his royal ancestors.

Genealogies were also important to the religious life of the people. A priest could not serve unless he could trace his ancestry back to Levi. Genealogy was also important to secure property rights. Land could not be sold permanently but it could be sold temporarily and genealogy was the way to guarantee that the land returned to the family every seventh year. And genealogy was important to establish identity. This was your identity: you came from a certain tribe and a certain clan and a certain family. Extended family ties were important, because a tribe cares for its members. And it was critical that the Messiah be born of the house and lineage of David.

There were many noble men in Joseph's family line: Abraham, Isaac, Jacob, Boaz, Obed, Jesse, as well as David, etc. As we have already noted there were also four notable woman of either questionable morals or questionable citizenship. Who were they? Tamar, Rahab, Ruth and the mother of Solomon (Bathsheba—remember, her name was omitted in the genealogy).

Technically, there is a slight problem with Jesus' genealogy. We read in Matthew 1:16: "**. . . and Jacob the father of Joseph, the husband of Mary, and Mary was the mother of Jesus** who is called the Messiah."

If Joseph was not really the father of Jesus, how can we say that Jesus was a descendant of David? Scholars tell us it is a matter of Jewish custom and practice.

Joseph took Mary, and the child whom she was carrying into his home and accepted all responsibility for them. According to Rabbinic law, when he did this he became the legal father of the child. Note also that Joseph, in obedience to the angel, gave the child its name, Jesus. According to Jewish law, he who names a child is reckoned as its father. So, in every way that matters, legally Joseph was Jesus' father. But, again, we are getting ahead of our story.

It was not until after her time with Elizabeth that Mary returned to Nazareth and confronted Joseph with the news that she was pregnant.

Mary and Joseph were betrothed to be married. According to the Jewish marriage customs at that time, Mary and Joseph's parents probably had arranged the match, with Joseph giving a sum of money called a *mohar* to Mary's father to secure her hand in marriage. Then, the engaged couple entered a formal 12 month betrothal. This time was considered as sacred as the marriage itself. Only a formal divorce could dissolve it. A written contract usually sealed the arrangement, and unfaithfulness constituted a moral breach; it was considered as adultery and was punishable by death.

The contract was marked by gifts given to the bride's parents and was accompanied by a feast of celebration. This was the first step in the marriage process (the last step was actual consummation between husband and wife), and was almost as binding as a marriage.

Traditionally, after the contract was signed, the bridegroom went home to prepare a place for his wife and returned at some undetermined time after the twelfth month to claim his bride, consummate the marriage, and bring her home.

The betrothal period, like our engagement period, was probably a time of hope and expectations. The couple dreamed of their lives together and of the future family they would create. This is the stage of seeing everything through rose-colored glasses. Mary and Joseph didn't get to experience this phase for very long, because some unexpected news would soon create a crisis in their relationship.

Mary's pregnancy during the betrothal period was a big surprise. Did Mary try to explain her situation to Joseph? How would she have done it? Did she make his favorite meal first? Was Joseph heartbroken? Did he retreat into his work? It had to be a very difficult time for him. It had to affect his feelings for Mary.

It reminds me of a true story about a man in South Carolina who was in the doghouse with his wife. He wanted to make amends, so he ordered her some flowers and told the florist that the card should read, "I'm sorry. I love you."

Evidently, his instructions were not clear enough. When the flowers arrived, there was no comma. The card read, "I'm sorry I love you."

That's a good way to make a bad situation worse. But that is probably how Joseph felt at first—sorry that he loved Mary.

Think of the shame that Mary and Joseph both would have endured if the news of Mary's pregnancy had gotten out.

The penalty for fornication or adultery was stoning, so theoretically, Mary could have been put to death for being pregnant out of wedlock. Joseph, who is described as a righteous man, not only does not have her stoned, he doesn't even want to publicly humiliate her. He wants to break their engagement quietly, so as not to shame her family.

Joseph showed himself at this juncture to be a loving and sympathetic man. He never let his offended ego get in the way. Many people when they are hurt try to hurt back. As John Maxwell says, "hurting people, hurt people." But not Joseph. All the power to punish Mary was in his hands, and he never chose that route.

An angel appears to Joseph while he is sleeping and explains the situation. We read in Matthew 1:20-23: "an angel of the Lord appeared to him in a dream and said, 'Joseph son of David, do not be afraid to take Mary home as your wife, because what is conceived in her is from the Holy Spirit. She will give birth to a son, and you are to give him the name Jesus, because he will save his people from their sins.'"

Then, we read these beautiful words in verses 24 and 25, "when Joseph woke up, he did what the angel of the Lord had commanded him and took Mary home as his wife. But he did not consummate their marriage until she gave birth to a son. And he gave him the name Jesus."

What a beautiful example of faith in God and faith in his beloved wife-to-be. He was commanded to take Mary home as his wife and that is exactly what he did. And he didn't look back.

At least two other times when the angel appears to Joseph—to tell him to take the family and flee to Egypt, and later when the angel instructed him to take the family back to Israel—the Bible reports that Joseph responded with immediate, unquestioning obedience. It is evident from the Biblical record that Joseph was a man of character, and that he loved God and he loved his wife. There is every reason to believe that the subject of Mary's premature pregnancy never came up again.

It's interesting. In spite of these stories concerning the question of Mary's pregnancy, nowhere in the New Testament record is Jesus' parentage ever questioned. He frequently read the Scriptures in the synagogues (Luke 4:16), a privilege strictly forbidden to illegitimate children (Deuteronomy 23:2). I wonder if this doesn't speak well of Mary and Joseph's reputation in the community. They were so well thought of that people didn't pay attention to the problem of the calendar.

Every young couple faces challenges in the first few years of their marriage. Sadly, many marriages fall apart, because the husband and wife don't have a shared vision of their future. They don't have any overriding principle that unifies them. God had given Mary and Joseph a shared vision of their future, a shared vision of the awesome role their son would play in ushering in the kingdom of God. This shared vision allowed them to look beyond the stress of present circumstance.

Now, let's go back to Luke's telling of the story, Luke 2.

In the last few months of Mary's pregnancy, a census decree went out. All the people must return to their hometown to be registered. In Joseph's case, this was Bethlehem—which fulfilled a prophecy of the birthplace of the Messiah. We have already noted the significance of Bethlehem in the biblical story. Returning for this registration could not have been a happy prospect for Joseph. He was confronted with a new tax to pay and a lengthy trip for his bride who was "heavy with child," as the King James Version put it.

The couple arrived in Bethlehem to discover the town was packed with visitors registering for the census. In a breach of Middle Eastern etiquette, there was no place to stay. Mary and Joseph stayed in a stable (probably a cave), where Mary gave birth.

Not long after Jesus' birth, shepherds came to worship the child. These shepherds confirmed the angel's promises to Mary and Joseph: their child is Messiah, the anointed one, sent from God to save all people. After eight days, he would have been circumcised according to Jewish law, and given his name. Accordingly he was given the name Jesus following the instructions that the angel had given to Mary in Luke 1:31, and Joseph in Matthew 1:21.

We learn more about Mary and Joseph's social station in life in Luke 1 when they take their newborn son to the Temple to make a thank offering to the Lord. In Leviticus 12: 6-8, instructions are given as to the proper sacrifice that must be made at the birth of a son. A lamb is the most acceptable sacrifice. But the poorest of families are allowed to substitute a lesser animal. The smallest acceptable sacrifice was two turtle doves, or pigeons. This is the sacrifice that Mary and Joseph offered to celebrate Jesus' birth.

While at the Temple, Mary and Joseph and their baby encounter Simeon a man who has been promised "by the Holy Spirit that he would not die before he had seen the Lord's Messiah." When he sees the babe, he exclaims, "sovereign Lord, as you have promised, you may now dismiss your servant in peace. For my eyes have seen your salvation . . ."

They also encounter a prophetess named Anna who "spoke about the child to all who were looking forward to the redemption of Jerusalem."

After this, we read that Joseph and Mary took Jesus and "returned into Galilee, to their own city Nazareth" (Luke 2:39).

Now, we return to Matthew's Gospel. It is there that we encounter the story of the magi's visit to this young family. Tradition tells us there were three of them, though the biblical record does not really say that. All we know is that they presented the newborn King with gifts of gold, frankincense, and myrrh. Perhaps Joseph used the proceeds from the sale of these gifts to fund their subsequent flight to Egypt.

The reason they had to flee to Egypt was because of a ruthless monarch known as Herod the great. Herod learned of the prophesied birth of this newborn "King of the Jews" from the magi during their search. Herod flew into a rage. He was obviously threatened by reports that a newborn baby would replace him as king. He sent men to murder all the infants age two and under in the region.

In his history of the period, Josephus says nothing about this slaughter by Herod, although no one denies that Herod was capable of such a thing. Herod was a thoroughly evil and violent man. For example, when he first came to power, Herod murdered the entire Sanhedrin.

Herod was not exactly a family man. He was married to ten women. He had fifteen children. Ten of them were boys. As his ten sons grew up and became men, they were destined to become king. Herod did not trust his sons and he accused two of them of treason. In the year 7 B.C., these two sons were sent back to Rome, put on trial, and assassinated at their daddy's order. In 4 B.C., Herod also killed his oldest son.

No wonder that Caesar Augustus said of Herod, "it is better to be Herod's pig than Herod's son." The quotation is a play on words. In Greek, which cultivated Romans spoke at the time, the word for pig (*hys*) and son (*hyios*) sound alike. "It is better to be Herod's *hys* than Herod's *hyios*."

Herod was a monster when he began his reign. He was a monster still at the very end. He knew that he would not be mourned when he died, so he arranged for a large number of people to be rounded up in Jerusalem and executed on that same day as well so there would mourners all around. The order, which would have ended the lives of three hundred or so of Jerusalem's citizens, was not carried out, but that was Herod's intent. So it is entirely consonant with his character to have all these infants slain rather than take the risk that one of them might grow up to challenge his throne.

After the death of Herod, Joseph brings his family back to Israel, to the town of Nazareth, which also fulfilled an Old Testament prophecy about the Messiah.

After this point there is no further mention of Joseph by name, although the story of Jesus in the Temple, in Jesus' 12th year, includes a reference to "both his parents." We do not know when Joseph died, but we see no mention of him after this journey to Jerusalem. He is not mentioned as being present with Mary at the wedding at Cana when Jesus turned the water to wine nor at the Passion at the end. According to Jewish custom, if he had been present at the Crucifixion, he would have been expected to take charge of Jesus' body, but this role is instead performed by Joseph of Arimathea. Nor would Jesus have entrusted his mother to John's care had Joseph been alive.

Have you ever thought of Mary as a single mom with a large family? After Jesus, she had four other sons (James, Joses, Judas,

Simon) and some daughters. We know this because they are mentioned in Mark's Gospel. Members of the family were also recorded as being active in the early church after Christ's Ascension.

Perhaps this is why Jesus waited until the age of thirty to begin his ministry. As the oldest son, he had responsibilities after Joseph's death. But think of the many difficulties that faced Mary as a single mom.

We see, in the course of Jesus' ministry, that Mary was not among Jesus' closest followers. They were close personally, but his work sometimes got in the way of his relationship with his family. In fact, at one point, Jesus' family was scandalized by His actions, and they asked him to return home.

But Mary is one of the faithful few who were brave enough to stand at the foot of the cross during Jesus' crucifixion along with "the disciple whom Jesus loved," Mary of Clopas and Mary Magdalene (John 19:25-26). Apparently, she was counted as one of His followers after His death. Acts 1:14 lists Mary among those people who awaited the coming of Jesus' Holy Spirit after the Ascension.

There is no evidence that Mary ever remarried. Roman Catholics have put Mary on a pedestal, in which she was permanently chaste. They explain the mention of Jesus' brothers and sisters as being the result of an earlier marriage by Joseph in which he was widowed. In our estimation, that is going too far, but that is a matter of faith.

We know that Jesus loved Mary. At his death, Jesus said to his beloved disciple, John, "Son, behold your mother." And then to Mary, "Mother, behold your son." There are some scholars who believe that Mary lived in exile with John on the island of Patmos before her death. It was there that John authored the book of Revelation.

To recap some of the joys and challenges of Mary and Joseph's relationship: they were an older husband and a younger wife. During their betrothal, a seeming breach of trust threatened to end their relationship and expose them to shame. Then, they received a shared, miraculous vision from God. They began married life in near-poverty. They received joyful confirmation from strangers of their son's special standing. They made a frightening escape from a murderous king, and had to start over in a foreign land. Eventually, they returned to their homeland, where they raised their son as a devout Jew. And finally, after Joseph's death, Mary became a single mom who didn't always understand her son, but always loved him and stood by him until the end.

The story of Mary and Joseph is as close to a modern love story as we find in Scriptures. There was mutual respect, amazing trust, and a deep religious faith–just the kind of parents to produce the King of Kings.

It reminds me of a story that was carried years ago in *The New York Times* about former Chief Justice of the Supreme Court, Earl Warren.

This was during the time of the Cuban missile crisis some 50 years ago.

Two thousand of the most important people in the government were issued laminated passes, with gold wire threaded through their ID photos to prevent counterfeiting. These imposing cards provided entry in a crisis, to the alternate seats of Government, a cavernous nuclear bomb shelter dug into a rural Virginia mountainside. Among the windowless offices stretching down its long fluorescent corridors were quarters for the Supreme Court, and among the passes were nine for the justices. But when officials came to the Court to give Chief Justice Earl Warren his pass, he remarked that he did not notice a pass for Mrs. Warren.

"Well, ah, there's not room for, um, wives," he was told, only for "very important people."

"Well, in that case," he said, "now you have room for another V.I.P.," as smiling, he handed his pass back.

Earl Warren wasn't going anywhere without his wife.

Joseph had that same kind of devotion to Mary and she to him. Perhaps you have experienced that kind of love. Perhaps you thought you had that kind of relationship with your partner, and you were badly hurt. Still, it is the ideal for most of us. Why? Because that kind of love reflects the heart of God. It is the kind of relationship for which we were created.

THE WORLD'S ONLY PERFECT HUSBAND
Revelation 19-22

The Rev. Jerry Anderson was at one time my pastor, and until his death a few years back, one of my closest friends. Jerry was an amazing story teller. My favorite "Jerry" story was of a wedding he once conducted. The setting for the wedding was beside a beautiful lake. Nearby, a lodge stood overlooking a shallow cove. On the porch of the lodge was an organ from a nearby church. Inside the lodge, the guests were enjoying refreshments and renewing old friendships.

At the appointed hour the 70-year-old organist, who had just finished her third martini, began playing with great enthusiasm. Out across the lake, motors roared as boats drifted into the cove, where the occupants lounged on deck to see what was going on. They were good old boys, drinking beer and sunning without their shirts. A blue haze rose from the motors as they circled the cove.

The service that the bride and groom chose was actually rather traditional, with one exception. The couple had devised their own innovative way of symbolizing their wedding covenant.

Close by, were two boxes holding white pigeons. The bride and groom, each having placed the ring on the finger of the other, was to release one of the pigeons to symbolize their union. All seemed in order, except for one small detail. The pigeons had been raised in pens and had never before flown!

When the groom tossed his bird into the air, it flew frantically into the tree where it fastened itself to a limb and hung fluttering upside down just above the pastor's head.

When the bride released her pigeon, it did two rollovers and landed in the lap of one of the grandmothers. The bird, confused and frightened, fastened its talons deep into grandmother's leg just above the knee. Her shrieks for help echoed across the lake. People rushed forward to rescue her.

After the sacred rite was completed, the bride, seemingly oblivious to everything that had happened, offered this comment: "This has been the most beautiful day I have ever known." [37]

I guess love really is blind. Nevertheless, weddings are almost always beautiful. We could only wish that every marriage was as beautiful as the wedding that preceded it.

If you are a man, you probably saw the title of this chapter, "The World's Only Perfect Husband" and wondered if I spelled your name right. Actually, I thought about naming you, but your wife set me right.

It may surprise you to know that there has only been one perfect husband. If you guessed Jesus Christ, you are right. We said at the beginning of this collection of great love stories that there really is only one truly *great* love story in the Bible . . . God's love for God's people. In the New Testament that love is echoed in Christ's love for his bride.

But you say, "I thought. Jesus never married." Oh, but he did. Go with me to the book of Revelation to verse 19:7, "Let us be glad and rejoice and honor him; for the time has come for the wedding banquet of the Lamb, and his bride has prepared herself."

Who is the Lamb? Christ. Who is the bride? The church.

The theme continues, "I saw the Holy City, the new Jerusalem, coming down out of heaven from God, prepared as a bride beautifully dressed for her husband . . ." (Rev. 21:2)

Then, in the last chapter of our Bible, we read, "The Spirit and the bride say, 'Come!' And let him who hears say, 'Come!'" (Rev. 22:17) So, in the very last chapter of scripture, describing the end of time we have this magnificent picture of Christ with his bride saying to all, "Come, come to the wedding feast. Come, all who would, and receive what has been prepared for you from the beginning of the world." This imagery is present in many of the parables that Jesus taught. We are the brides of Christ. We are his beloved. And one day we will join him at the wedding feast.

There is no sweeter or more beautiful picture of the wedding of Christ and his bride than that provided by Joni Eareckson Tada in her book, *When Morning Gilds the Skies*. Hopefully, you know Joni's story already:

As a teenager, Joni Eareckson loved life. She enjoyed riding horses, hiking, tennis, and loved to swim. On Sunday, July 30, 1967 everything changed. While on a beach outing, Joni dove into Chesapeake Bay not knowing how shallow the water was. She broke her neck—a fracture between the fourth and fifth cervical levels—and became a quadriplegic, paralyzed from the shoulders down.

Now Joni was fighting for her life and facing the fact that she would have to live the rest of her life in a wheelchair. Her rehabilitation was not easy, and she struggled through it for the next two years. She was angry, struggled with depression, and had frequent thoughts of suicide. Joni questioned how God let this happen to her. But as she participated in various rehabilitation programs that taught her how to live with her disabilities, she also immersed herself in the scriptures that she might become spiritually strong. Today she is an inspiration to millions of people.

Since those early days of struggle with her physical condition, Joni has written forty-eight books, recorded several musical albums, starred in a major autobiographical movie of her life, and is actively involved as an advocate for disabled people. During her two years of rehabilitation, Joni even learned to paint with a brush between her teeth, and later began selling her artwork. [38]

In 1982 she married a teacher, Ken Tada. Her description of their wedding is most striking. She describes the difficulty in getting dressed for the day as well as the challenges of navigating a wheel chair while wearing a voluminous wedding gown. She says she decidedly didn't feel like the picture-perfect bride you see in magazines. That is, she didn't feel much like a beautiful bride until she looked into the eyes of Ken, her soon-to-be husband. And then she says everything changed. Suddenly she was the pure and perfect bride. *Why?* Because in Ken's eyes she saw herself bathed in love.

She wrote, "I think heaven will be a little like that . . . [We] fix our eyes on Jesus . . . On that glorious Day, all He'll see is our 'fine linen, bright and clean.' All He'll see is His beautiful bride. And one look from Him will change us forever. All the stains of earthly life will be purified away just by one searching of those eyes. Our faces will flush, our hearts will pound, for it will be more than we ever dreamed of, more than we ever longed for. And at the sight of our Bridegroom we just might sing . . . 'In mansions of glory and endless delight, I'll ever adore thee in heaven so bright; I'll sing with the glittering crown on my brow: If ever I loved thee, my Jesus, 'tis now.'" [39]

That's Joni's testimony. Who wouldn't look forward to that kind of wedding ceremony as we stand before the throne of God?

I grew up in the Church Street Methodist Church in Knoxville, Tennessee. Church Street Church is a large gothic structure in the heart of downtown Knoxville. It features fifty-eight magnificent stained glass windows designed by the renowned stained glass artist Charles J. Connick. It is in every way a place of reverence and beauty. Even to this day, the music is traditional church music accompanied by a ninety-one rank Aeolian-Skinner Pipe Organ. Bach and Beethoven are as much a part of the worship as the hymns of Charles and John Wesley.

That's my background, though I confess that I now prefer so-called "contemporary worship." I clap and sway with praise songs to the sound of guitars and drums. But there is a part of me that grieves the fact that my grandchildren will probably never sing the great hymns of the church that I sang at Church Street. It's partly my fault, since I wandered off to a more modern style of worship, but still it's sad.

One of the hymns that we sang quite regularly at Church Street and that still occupies a special place in my heart is the hymn, "The Church's One Foundation [is Jesus Christ her Lord]." The verse I remember best goes like this "From heaven he came and sought her to be his holy bride, with his own blood he bought her and for her life he died."

I don't know why the image of the church, as Christ's bride, fascinated me as a young person, but it did—and it still does today.

Actually, the idea of the "divine marriage" is not unique to the New Testament. It appears quite often, and with much beauty and power in the Hebrew Bible [the Old Testament] as well.

We've already seen it in the story of Hosea and Gomer.

However, one of the most powerful examples occurs in Ezekiel 16. The New International Version of the Bible tells the story like this. *And please don't skim over this passage; it is a wonderful piece of scripture, which often goes unnoticed.*

The word of the LORD came to me: "Son of man, confront Jerusalem with her detestable practices and say, 'this is what the Sovereign LORD says to Jerusalem: Your ancestry and birth were in the land of the Canaanites; your father was an Amorite and your mother a Hittite. On the day you were born your cord was not cut, nor were you washed with water to make you clean, nor were you rubbed with salt or wrapped in cloths. No one looked on you with pity or had compassion enough to do any of these things for you. Rather, you were thrown out into the open field, for on the day you were born you were despised.

"'Then, I passed by and saw you kicking about in your blood, and as you lay there in your blood I said to you, "Live!" I made you grow like a plant of the field. You grew and developed and entered puberty. Your breasts had formed and your hair had grown, yet you were stark naked.

"'Later, I passed by, and when I looked at you and saw that you were old enough for love, I spread the corner of my garment over you and covered your naked body. I gave you my solemn oath and entered into a covenant with you,' declares the Sovereign LORD, 'and you became mine.

"'I bathed you with water and washed the blood from you and put ointments on you. I clothed you with an embroidered dress and put sandals of fine leather on you. I dressed you in fine linen and covered you with costly garments. I adorned you with jewelry: I put bracelets on your arms and a necklace around your neck, and I put a ring on your nose, earrings on your ears and a beautiful crown on your head. So you were adorned with gold and silver; your clothes were of fine linen and costly fabric and embroidered cloth. Your food was honey, olive oil, and the finest flour. You became very beautiful and rose to be a queen. And your fame spread among the nations on account of your beauty, because the splendor I had given you made your beauty perfect,' declares the Sovereign Lord . . . ."

Wow! Can there be a more beautiful picture of grace than that? God found his beloved people when they were despised, rejected and "covered with blood" and loved them and made them His bride. Of course, Ezekiel goes on to describe in similarly graphic terms Israel's unfaithfulness to the God who had loved them so much, "You adulterous wife! You prefer strangers to your own husband . . ." God says (v. 32), and Israel is punished for its sin. However, the metaphor is still striking. God loves His people in the same way that Hosea loved Gomer his unfaithful wife, but with an everlasting love that cannot be destroyed.

We see the same imagery in Isaiah 62:1-5.

Israel is in a bad way. Time after time, their enemies had defeated them. They were recovering from exile in Babylonia. The land is deserted and desolate. Jerusalem has been torn down and the temple has been destroyed. There is a phrase that is often used about the prophets—that they afflict the comfortable and comfort the afflicted. Isaiah is in his comforting mode in this passage and here is the word he gives Israel in God's behalf: "You shall no more be termed Forsaken, and your land shall no more be termed Desolate; but you shall be called, *My Delight Is in Her*, and your land Married; for the Lord delights in you, and your land shall be married. For as a young man marries a young woman, so shall your builder marry you, and as the bridegroom rejoices over the bride, so shall your God rejoice over you." (62:4-5)

The word "married" is important. There were negative cultural connotations to a woman who was not married in those ancient times. An unmarried woman was often an outcast, and widows lived an uncertain existence. Since women could not own property, if a woman had no family, it was almost impossible for her to provide for herself above the most meager of existences without resorting to prostitution. So, once Israel was abandoned and desolate, says Isaiah, but now she has two significant new names "My delight" and "Married." It is a beautiful way of expressing God's love and God's grace. Maybe you've gone through a difficult time when your name could easily have been, "Abandoned" and "Desolate." Then this passage is for you.

The concept of the divine marriage was a familiar one to the Jews. The New Testament church applied that same concept to Christ's relationship to the church. Paul even used this imagery in advising couples about their own marriages. He wrote in Ephesians 5:

25-33,

"Husbands, love your wives, just as Christ loved the church and gave himself up for her to make her holy, cleansing her by the washing with water through the word, and to present her to himself as a radiant church, without stain or wrinkle or any other blemish, but holy and blameless. In this same way, husbands ought to love their wives as their own bodies. He who loves his wife loves himself. After all, no one ever hated their own body, but they feed and care for their body, just as Christ does the church—for we are members of his body. 'For this reason, a man will leave his father and mother and be united to his wife, and the two will become one flesh.' This is a profound mystery—but I am talking about Christ and the church. However, each one of you also must love his wife as he loves himself, and the wife must respect her husband."

This is marriage at its best—mutual love, respect, and faithfulness.

Sonja Ely was watching her five-year-old granddaughter play with her toys. At one point, her granddaughter staged a wedding, first playing the role of the mother-of-the-bride assigning specific duties in the wedding ceremony, then suddenly becoming the bride herself with her "teddy-bear" as her groom.

As the make-believe wedding moved toward the high point, her granddaughter picked her teddy-bear groom up and said to the imaginary minister presiding over the wedding, "now you can read us our rights."

Without missing a beat, she then became the minister who said, "You have the right to remain silent, anything you say may be held against you, you have the right to have an attorney present. You may kiss the bride." [40]

This sounds like the recipe for many marriages today, doesn't it? Many people today need help with their marriages. I would not presume to know all the answers for making a marriage work. Still, there are some factors that seem to be present in most of the successful marriages we've seen in these great love stories from the Bible.

For one thing, successful couples share certain values. This does not mean that our spouse should be a carbon copy of ourselves. That was never God's intent. We see this in that very first story—of

Adam and Eve. When in Genesis 2:18 we read: "I will make a helper suitable for him," the Hebrew word for "suitable" literally translates to "opposite." So, it's all right sometimes if, "opposites attract." Differences are appropriate and good. However, unless there are areas of life where there is some overlap, then a major source of strength is absent from the marriage. This is particularly true in the area of values. Successful couples have shared values.

Usually, they share the same values with regard to involvement in church and in the raising of their children as well as the use of money. One of the values they share in common is a commitment to be faithful to one another.

The media often give us a distorted view of the so-called mores of our society. Would it surprise you that a Gallup poll, commissioned by *Self* magazine early in the nineties, reported that a large majority of married men say they wouldn't have an affair, even if they were certain their loved one would never find out?

This was a survey of all men—it was not restricted to those who go to church. Of 500 men surveyed, 67% of married men say an affair is absolutely out of the question. Only 5% of married men said outright they would have an affair. The rest said maybe.

It simply is not true, regardless of what you see on television or in Washington that we are an adulterous society. Overall, we are a people who treasure fidelity. By the way, here's an interesting tidbit: 95% of married men say they wouldn't drop their partner for a trophy wife if they became extremely successful or wealthy. [41] If you are a wife, you may be relieved—unless, of course, you were planning on acquiring a trophy husband.

Regardless of what you might find reported in the media, faithfulness in marriage is as important to most people as it has ever been. Unfaithfulness is a violation of the promise you made to your spouse before God. Successful couples have shared values. They also have mutual respect.

Two old friends were playing a round of golf together. One of them was taking an especially long time to tee off; checking the wind, checking his grip, measuring the distance, changing his stance, fiddling around with the tee, looking up, looking down, looking all around, and then starting the routine all over again whenever distracted by a car, chirping bird, flowing stream, or his friend's breathing. Finally, his exasperated friend screamed, "What's taking so long? Just hit the dang ball for cryin' out loud!"

"But my wife is watching me from the clubhouse," the man explained, "and I want to make sure it's a perfect shot."

His friend said, "Forget it! She's too far away! You'll never hit her from here!" [42]

We joke about marriage. We always joke about things that are important to us, but a central theme of successfully married couples is that they respect one another. Successful couples listen to one another. They pay attention to one another's hopes and dreams.

There was an interesting—if somewhat gruesome item in the news sometime back. Margarita Sanchez of Huatusco, Mexico, slept next to the body of her dead husband for eight days. She did not know he was dead. She thought he was simply ignoring her. [43]

Imagine that. They did not communicate for eight days, and she did not think it out of the ordinary. That could happen to one degree or another in many marriages.

Successful couples listen to one another and prize one another's insights. And even though there are some significant areas in life where they disagree, they listen and they value the exchange.

Successful couples, above all, are committed to making their marriage work. Time and again this is what surveys tell us is critical to a lasting marriage—both partners are committed to the marriage.

One evening a man was very impressed with the meat entree his wife had served. "What did you marinate this in?" he asked.

His wife immediately went into a long explanation about how much she loves him and how life wouldn't be the same without him. Eventually, his puzzled expression made her interrupt her answer with a question of her own.

"What did you ask me?" she asked. She chuckled at his answer and explained, "I thought you asked me if I would marry you again!"

As she left the room, he called out, "well, would you marry me again?"

Without hesitation, she replied, "vinegar and barbecue sauce." [44]

Would she marry him again? Most married people say, "yes." But many marriages wither and die because there is not a commitment on the part of both partners to make the marriage last.

Maybe you know the story of Isidor and Ida Straus. They were passengers on the ill-fated maiden voyage of the Titanic. Ida refused at least two opportunities to escape the sinking ship, choosing instead to die with her husband of 41 years, a well-known philanthropist who owned Macy's department store.

News that the couple had shared their fate came as no surprise to their six children and many friends. "When they were apart, they wrote to each other every day," says Joan Adler, director of the Straus Historical Society. "She called him 'my darling papa.' He called her 'my darling momma.' For years they had even celebrated their different birthdays on the same day."

As the Titanic went down, Ida, 63, resisted the pleas of officers to climb into a lifeboat, insisting instead that her maid take her place. She handed the young woman her fur coat. "I won't need this anymore," she said. She was finally cajoled into boarding the second-to-last lifeboat, only to clamber out again as Isidor, 67, stepped away.

Last seen clasped in an embrace, Ida and Isidor are memorialized in a Bronx cemetery with a monument inscribed, "Many waters cannot quench love, and neither can the floods drown it." [45]

We need to understand in this day of uncertain relationships that there are relationships like that. There are couples who love one another in the same way that Christ loved his bride, the church.

While serving aboard a gunboat in Vietnam, Dave Roever was holding a phosphorus grenade some six inches from his face when a sniper's bullet ignited the explosive. In his book, *Welcome Home, Davey*, he describes the first time he saw his face after the explosion, "when I looked in that mirror, I saw a monster, not a human being . . . My soul seemed to shrivel up and collapse in on itself, to be sucked into a black hole of despair. I was left with an indescribable and terrifying emptiness. I was alone in the way the souls in hell must feel alone." Finally Roever came back to the States to meet with his young bride, Brenda.

Just before Brenda arrived, Roever watched the wife of another burn victim tell her husband that she wanted a divorce. Then Brenda walked in.

"Showing not the slightest tremor of horror or shock," Roever writes, "she bent down and kissed me on what was left of my face. Then she looked me in my good eye, smiled, and said, 'Welcome home,

Davey! I love you.' To understand what that meant to me you have to know that's what she called me when we were most intimate; she would whisper 'Davey,' over and over in my ear . . . By using her term of endearment for me, she said, You are my husband. You will always be my husband. You are still my man." [46]

I can hear Christ say that to us in all our ugliness and sin, not because of who we are, but because of who he is . . . and his great love for us, his bride.

A few years ago, there was a man whose wife became seriously ill with Alzheimer's disease. She completely lost all of her memory and her ability to remember who she was or who anyone else was. She was in a nursing home and her husband came by to sit beside her bed and be beside her every day.

One of his sons told him that he didn't need to do that because she didn't remember who she was and she didn't remember who he was.

The man said, "I know she doesn't remember anything, but I do. I remember who she is and I remember who I am. I am the husband who said to her 55 years ago, 'I will love and cherish you for better or worse and in sickness and health.' And I intend to do just that." [47]

Who loves us that much? If you haven't found someone who loves you like that, I hope you will. But I do know someone who loves you like that. From the beginning to the end of the Bible, there is one great love story. It is the story of God's love for you and me and for everyone on this earth. It is the story of Christ who sacrificed his life for his bride, the church. And one day we will be joined with him and all the saints at the great wedding feast of God.

Notes

INTRODUCTION

1. Attributed to David Learn, http://www.mail-archive. com/timothy@topica.com/msg00045.html.

CHAPTER ONE

2. http://www.chucksmoot.net/sermons-power.html.

3. Anthony Evans, *Preaching Today*

4. David A. Macleod "Life in These United States," *Reader's Digest,* Feb. 2002, p. 218.

5. Rev. Rob Perkins, http://www.newtonpres.org/learn_more/ sermon_pdfs/Sermon_102801.pdf.

CHAPTER TWO

6. Douglas Jerrold, Leo Rosten's *Giant Book of Laughter* (New York: Bonanza Books, 1985).

7. Sue Monk Kidd, *When the Heart Waits*, (San Francisco: Harper San Francisco, 1990), p. 22.

8. Bruce Feiler, *Abraham, A Journey to the Heart of Three Faiths* (William Morrow, 2002), p. 66-67

9. Cited at http://www.sermonnotebook.org/romans/ Rom%204_18-25.htm..

10. help4sunday@psst. com (Help 4 Sunday)

CHAPTER THREE

11. "In Their Own Words." By Capt. Gordon Sparks, *The Asbury Herald,* Volume 112, No. 2 & 3, p. 11.

12. "On a Wild and Windy Mountain," by William H. Willimon, *Pulpit Resource,* April/May/June 1996, p. 54.

13. *Romancing The Home: How to Have a Marriage That Sizzles* (Broadman & Holman Publishers, 1993).

14. "Secrets of a Long and Happy Marriage," *USA Today*, Sept. 1992, p. 4.

CHAPTER FOUR

15. Jim Pietsch, *The New York City Cab Driver's Joke Book*, (New York, Warner Brothers, 1998).

16. Interview with Claudia Dreifus in *Modern Maturity*, March-April 1997.

17. Paul Harvey, *The Rest of the Story*, p. 84. Cited in *Bits and Pieces*, Oct, 1990

18. H. C. Leupold, *Exposition of Genesis* (Grand Rapids: Baker Book House, 1942), II, p. 811.

19. By Thomas F. Crum, in Jack Canfield, Mark Victor Hansen, Mark and Chrissy Donnelly, and Barbara DeAngelis, Ph.D. *Chicken Soup for the Couple's Soul* (Deerfield Beach, FL.: Health Communications, 1999), pp. 113-114.

CHAPTER FIVE

20. (New York: Simon & Schuster, 1983) pp. 167-168.

CHAPTER SIX

21. Rodney Jones and Gerald Uelmen, *Supreme Folly* (New York: W.W. Norton & Company, Inc., 1990), pp. 151-153.

22. As recorded by Michael Martin Murphey. © 2004 Smith Music Group.

23. James W. Moore, *When All Else Fails . . . Read The Instructions* (Nashville: Dimensions for Living, 1993), pp. 32-33.

24. Stan Mooneyham, *Dancing On The Strait & Narrow* (San Francisco: Harper & Row, Publishing, 1989), pp. 34-35.

25. Virginia Duran, "Someday, You'll Do As Much," *Guideposts*, May 1994, pp. 16-19.

CHAPTER SEVEN
26. Frederick Buechner, *The Clown In The Belfry* (San Francisco: HarperSanFrancisco, 1992), pp. 115-116.

CHAPTER EIGHT
27. Christine Wicker. *God Knows My Heart* (New York: St. Martin's Press, 1999), p. 28.

28. Gary Richmond, *A View from the Zoo* (W Pub Group, 1987).

29. Lawrence O. Richards. *The 365-Day Devotional Commentary* (Colorado Springs, CO.: ChariotVictor Publishing, 1987), p. 533.

30. By Jay Bakker in *Stories of Emergence*, edited by Mike Yaconelli (Grand Rapids, Michigan: Zondervan, 2003), p. 182.

CHAPTER NINE
31. Leo Rosten, *The Joys Of Yinglish* (New York: McGraw-Hill Publishing Company, 1992

32. CNN.com, "Swazi women dance to catch king's eye," Aug 29, 2005. International Edition.

CHAPTER TEN
33. *The Word in Life Study Bible* (Nashville: Thomas Nelson Publishers, 1993), p. 206.

34. I drew inspiration for this story from a sermon by Rev. Frank Lyman in *Dynamic Preaching* magazine and from a Christmas monologue by Selina I. Duncan.

CHAPTER ELEVEN
35. Date unknown.

36. Richards, R. Scott. *Myths the World Taught Me* (Nashville: Thomas Nelson Publishers, 1991), 173.

CHAPTER TWELVE
37. Jerry Anderson, *Hollyhocks and Hummingbirds* (Knoxville, TN: Seven Worlds Publishing).

38. http://en.wikipedia.org/wiki/Joni_Eareckson_Tada.

39. Joni Eareckson Tada et al., *When Morning Gilds the Skies* (Wheaton: Crossway Books, 2002), pp. 22–25.

40. Edward K. Rowell, *Humor for Preaching and Teaching* (Grand Rapids: Baker Books, 1996).

41. *Reader's Digest*, August, 1982.

42. *U.S.A. Today*, May 26, 1992, p. D1.

43. "The 1998 Dubious Achievement Awards," *Esquire*, Jan., 1999, p. 87.

44. "Every Shot I Ever Hit," by Dr. Robert R. Kopp, Oct. 4, 1998, p. 1.

45. "Sunken Dreams," *People,* March 16, 1998, p. 47.

46. Dennis and Barbara Rainey, *Moments Together for Couples* (Ventura, California: Regal Books, 1995).

47. Dr. William S. Shillady, http://www.parkavemethodist.org/sermon.php?s=16.